The Disinherited

To Munira:
with fond geetings.

Fawaz Turki

The Disinherited

Journal of a
Palestinian Exile
by Fawaz Turki
With an Epilogue 1974

(MR) New York and London

Contents

Preface

The major source for this book is my own recollections of what we have endured and my own conviction that ours is a just cause, a cause long forgotten by the Western world (self-righteous in its overly easy conscience) and long mutilated by the Arab world (self-satisfied in its mercenary games).

Consequently this is not an objective work. It is however a sincere narration of a phase in the history of the Palestinian people and of their response to the challenge of adversity that has confronted them over the past two decades. As I lived that phase and took a part in that response, what I have to say, subjective though it is, may offer some notes toward an understanding of what we are doing now and an insight into the why and the how of it.

I am neither concerned nor qualified to indulge in the game of quote and counter-quote adopted by those whose business or ideology drives them to espouse the position of one or the other. I have discovered that with enough diligence, the historian can present a devastatingly convincing version of the Zionist/Israeli/Jewish (call it what you wish) claim in modern Palestine. Another historian, with equal reserves of diligence and partisan to our own claims and grievances, can come up with a perfectly valid and at the same time diametrically opposite view.

"The vexatious issue," as the problem of my people was called during the Truman and Mandate years, has now expanded and become the "Arab-Israeli" conflict; and it is felt that the solution of it by the big powers is as mandatory now as it was mandatory then.

Mine is not a vexatious issue, nor has it much to do with the conflict now raging between the Arabs and the Zionists. Nor is its solution dependent upon, nor will I allow it to be, the whims of the big powers. Mine is an existential problem having to do with the yearning for my homeland, with being part of a culture, with winning the battle to remain myself, as a Palestinian belonging to a people with a distinctly Palestinian consciousness.

If I was not a Palestinian when I left Haifa as a child, I am one now. Living in Beirut as a stateless person for most of my growing-up years, many of them in a refugee camp, I did not feel I was living among my "Arab brothers." I did not feel I was an Arab, a Lebanese, or, as some wretchedly pious writers claimed, a "southern Syrian." I was a Palestinian. And that meant I was an outsider, an alien, a refugee and a burden. To be that, for us, for my generation of Palestinians, meant to look inward, to draw closer, to be part of a minority that had its own way of doing and seeing and feeling and reacting. To be that, for us, meant the addition of a subtler nuance to the cultural makeup of our Palestinianness.

The experience of our growing-up years—blame that experience on the Arab governments, blame it on the UN, blame it on God, for the cabalistic interpretation of political events does not interest me—has decidedly ravished our beings. It ravished the law and the order of the reality that we saw around us. It defeated some of us. It reduced and distorted and alienated others.

The defeated, like myself, took off to go away from the intolerable pressures of the Arab world to India and Europe and Australia, where they wrestled with the problem and hoped to understand. The reduced, like my parents, waited helplessly in a refugee camp for the world, for a miracle, or for some deity to come to their aid. The distorted, like Sirhan Sirhan, turned into assassins. The alienated, like Leila Khaled, hijacked civilian aircraft.

If there are still people around who call us "Arab refugees" or "southern Syrians" or terrorists, who want to subdue us, who want to resettle us, who want to ignore us and who want to play games with our destiny, then they are not tuned in to the vibrations and the tempo of the Third World, of which the Palestinians are a part.

Every writer and speaker wants to win his audience to his point of view, a point of view that is carried along by the weight of its supposed impartiality. I have no point of view to make. And I cannot pretend to begin to be impartial.

When I was a child, a few weeks after we left Palestine in 1948, I used to sit with a crowd of people at the camp, mothers and fathers and aunts and grandparents and young wives and children, to listen to the radio at precisely three o'clock every day. The voice from Radio Israel (or Radio Tel Aviv, or whatever damn name it had) used to come on to announce The Messages. Silence would fill the space around us. Tension would grip even the children. "From Abu Sharef, and Jameela, Samir and Kamal in Haifa," the words would come across the air. "To our Leila and her husband Fouad. Are you in Lebanon? We are all well." A few moments pause, then: "From Abu and Um Shihadi, and Sofia and Osama to Abu Adib and his family. Is Anton with you? We are worried." The dispassionate voice continues: "From Ibrahim Shawki to his wife Zamzam. I have moved to Jaffa. Your father is safe with us."

One whole hour of this. During it an outburst of tears at the knowledge that loved ones are well. Despair that a relative is not yet located. Hope that in tomorrow's broadcast a good word may be heard. Then a trip on the bus to the Beirut station to queue up at the message office to send your own twenty-six words across the ether to the other side. Because you could not go over there yourself to say them. Because an armistice line was drawn as a consequence of a war you did not understand, did not want, did not initiate.

A few years later, we were still in that refugee camp on the outskirts of Beirut where life was becoming harder and existence becoming more futile. The Lebanese authorities, conscious of the image of their capital as a "Western city," made attempts to move our camp, as far away as they could, to avoid offending foreign visitors with the sight of it. Our camp was on the way to the airport.

For bureaucratic or other reasons, the initiative failed. But no one at the Ministry of the Interior, and no one in any editor's office, bothered to consider or write about the hardship we would have endured had we in fact been moved forty miles out of town. Or the disruption this might have caused in the lives of children going to school, men going to work, the sick going to their doctors, and the women going to their shops. Or the indignity to a people already devastated by one uprooting from their homeland.

The story of these years is thus not offered as a point of view. It is not written with objectivity. Nor in the telling do I hope to win adherents to my cause. I merely wish to isolate our problem from the Arab-Israeli dispute, identify it and describe it in its human dimensions, ·for those who wish to know what it was like, what it will be like.

The relentless and persistent falsification of facts by commentators, and the two-decade-long custody of our problem in the hands of the Arab governments, have created myths around who we were and what we wanted. We were the primitive Bedouins roaming the desert; we were an illiterate and disease-stricken mass of refugees packed in DP camps; we were the hateful, embittered Arabs—indistinguishable from other "Arabs"—who yearned to destroy Israel and "drive the Jews into the sea." We were the harmless villains of the piece, turned, at the end, into intractable ones.

Given their noisy pursuit of a commitment to Israel and the Zionist experiment, people in the West often blinded themselves to the truth and accepted these myths. Our problem, dehumanized, distorted, and twisted, was flogged into a state beyond recognition. Conversely, the creation of Israel became an experience and a monument. The Western world, which had long tormented and abused the Jewish people, hastened to bless an event that saw an end to their victims' suffering. A debt was to be paid. Who was to pay it and where it was to be paid were not seen as of the essence, so long as it was not paid by Europeans in Europe. After the pogroms in Czarist Russia and the crimes in Nazi Germany, for example, Great Britain and the United States, two countries that gave whole-hearted support to unrestricted Jewish emigration to Palestine and the creation of a "Jewish Home," were concurrently providing for legislation to control "alien entry" into their green and pleasant lands. This was but a manifestation of the style and vocabulary of the Social Darwinism they had for many years practiced in their rencontre with the "unfit" of the earth.

To illustrate this, I need only indulge in a recollection or two of the time I was in Palestine during the last years of the Mandate, as can any individual who has lived under a colonial system and experienced the "native" consciousness.

In the small township of Balad el-Sheikh, near Haifa, where we lived, I was returning home from school one day when I spotted an old man standing at a street corner peddling bread rolls from a tray on a wooden stand. Peddlers are a way of life in our part of the world, men who make and market their own products, unfettered by the structured patterns of a developed economy. Old men with gray hair, like the peddler in question, trying to make a living in a land that has long been ruled, exploited, oppressed, and manipulated by a succession of foreign occupiers.

A British soldier, a youngster with a machine-gun slung over his shoulder, crossed from the other side of the street, nonchalantly walked up to the peddler, and proceeded to beat him on the face and chest. Blows that he aimed, violently and indiscriminately, first with his fists, then with his weapon. When the old man fell to the ground, the soldier picked up the tray, threw it in the air, and then began to break the stand into pieces, hitting it against the wall and jumping on it. With that accomplished, he walked away. All this was done for no apparent, no warrantable, no explicable, reason.

But our English soldier no doubt felt that since there were only Englishmen and one other species of humans populating the earth, he had carte blanche to act as he wished. If by beating up a "native" he could "feel better," then he was entitled to do it. He was not answerable for his act. Not in Palestine; not in India; not in Africa. If he ran over a child with his army jeep, so long as it was a "native" child he need only reverse his vehicle and finish him off. (It happened to a cousin of mine.) If he was being transported overland from his old base to another one across the country, on a tedious trip of long duration, then he could take his gun, aim it, and shoot to death a "native" riding along on his mule, a "native" working in his fields, a "native" coming out of his hut. When this soldier returned home, to live again among his race of Englishmen, he would be chastised for kicking a dog, convicted in court for libeling a man, ostracized for indecent language. (But the world, the times, the English soldier, and I have changed since those days.)

So when Theodore Herzl, the European from Vienna, spoke of creating "a rampart of Europe, an outpost of civilization" against "Asian barbarism" in Palestine, no one came forth to oppose the concept and its execution. The event was applauded.

And it came about that within a short time after its creation at the cost of much misery to others, Israel began to enjoy and bask in the image of a land transformed from, as is often said, "the deserts and marshes of Palestine into the garden that is the Zionist state." Israel was beyond reproach. It had proved itself for the David that it was, surrounded by a monstrous Goliath dedicated to its destruction. There was no question of the integrity and innocence of Israel. There was no question either of who the villains of the region were. (It was too bad about "the Arab refugees"—who as recently as 1918 had formed 92 percent of the population of the country—but they had left voluntarily, opted to live in refugee camps and, at any rate, they too were the enemy. Resettlement of refugees was a picayune problem that remained unsolved because of Arab intransigence.)

The vast machinery of Zionist propaganda, with a great helping hand from Nasser and his fellow Arab leaders, to whom irresponsible pronunciamentos became a fetish, fostered and enhanced this image of a tiny Israel that deserved to continue its mission and its harmless endeavors in the face of the enemy. Everything with Israel that had been and that was is as it must be. Books with titles like *The Miracle in the Desert, Israel's Struggle for Survival,* and *Hope and Fulfillment* discussed the miracle in the desert, Israel's struggle for survival and hope and fulfillment. The Jewish and the Zionist causes were inextricably tied and seen as one.

The consequences of this blind faith in Israel and Israel's activities and intentions were extensive. The foundations of this image were little shaken when Israel blatantly allied itself with the imperialist powers in the 1956 tripartite aggression against Egypt. The massacre of Kafr Qassem in that same year, that senseless murder of fifty-one men, women, and children who were on their way home from the fields, was hardly reported in the Western press. More than that, little was written on how the Israeli government itself attempted to suppress the news of the massacre, or on the fact that when the news did ultimately surface and punishment was meted out in the courts, the convicted soldiers served a total of less than one year in jail (and on release some returned to serve in the government). The way the "niggers of Israel," as Hal Draper called the Palestinians living in Israel, were treated in their own homeland by the authorities and by Israeli society was never considered a subject that warranted debate or reporting.

The faults of Israel are not my problem. Let those who support it ponder them. But it has been a paradox of unfathomable dimensions to me, unable to experience the Western consciousness, to watch the spectacle of those commentators and activists who have proved themselves worthy of any liberal cause, any humanitarian endeavor, any opposition to oppression, any support for the liberation of colonized or persecuted minorities, yet who, vis-à-vis Israel, remain blind to, or brush aside evidence of, Israeli guilt of the same crimes they are themselves crusading against.

With pressures such as these and with the dividends Arab leaders such as Nasser have derived from co-opting our cause for their own nefarious purposes, the central issue that truly was the origin of the crisis, the Palestinian problem, has been lost to sight and sound.

Why this problem was allowed to come about in the first place is the business of the historian. He has a habit of tracing the development of every conflict, pinpointing where its seeds were planted, and endowing every subsequent event with immanent logic. He should be wished luck. For as I. F. Stone has suggested, if God is now truly dead, as some say he is, he undoubtedly died from trying to untangle the origins of the Middle East conflict.

But when and how this problem will be solved *is* our business. We have picked up our own habits, in this world, in this age of ours.

1. Flight

I am aware that I have been stateless for nearly all of my twenty-nine years; that I have lived and grown up in a refugee camp on the edge of the desert; that except for those freckle-nosed bureaucrats in the West who from time to time endorsed a shipment of food and warm blankets to me, I did not (for all men and for all they knew) exist on the face of this globe; that I was robbed of my sense of purpose and sense of worth as a human being and was forced to line up obsequiously outside UN food depots each month; and that when for two decades I feared, I feared only the cold of twenty winters, and when I dreamed, I dreamed only of the food that others ate. I am also aware that this knowledge has mutilated my reality and impoverished my consciousness; that I lived, as a million of my fellow Palestinians lived, silently walking hither and thither along the muddy paths of DP camps, in a void, in a state of non-being because everything had been taken away from us, including our tangible abstractions; and that as a result, our beings were engulfed at times by lunatic extremes of hate and bitterness and at others by frustrated resignation.

With our memories of places and times we had known before, rational and good, floating in the space around us and within us, we existed not in the present tense, the tense of reality, but the future imperfect, when next year, next time, next speech, the wrongs will have been righted, the grievances removed, and our cause justified. We lay, as it were, supine under a tree; but, in a world where men will calmly use historical reality to suit their own issues, Godot, for whom we waited, never arrived.

My generation of Palestinians, growing up alienated, excluded, and forgotten, rejected this legacy; yet when we looked around us we could see either the desert to shed our tears in or the whole world to hit back at. Having nothing and with nothing to lose, we proceeded to do the latter. But our struggle was for our place in history, our right to glimpse a vision, to search for hope, to return to Palestine. We struggled for the phoenix, not the phantom, that is our homeland. As de Tocqueville observed in his commentary on the forces that led to the French Revolution: "Patiently endured so long as it seemed beyond redress, a grievance comes to appear intolerable once the possibility of removing it crosses men's minds."

How did it come about that a whole nation found itself suddenly in exile and its two million people afflicted by defeat, hunger, and humiliation, repudiated by men, despised by host countries and forgotten by the world, left to live as pariah refugees, their disinherited souls empty of hope and devoid of meaning? How did it come about that they accepted with a stoic calm the vagaries of homelessness and the agonies of destitution? How did it come about that a versatile and ingenious people continued for many years to provoke, in their life-style and attitudes, identification with backwardness, illiteracy, stagnation, and an inability or unwillingness to transcend their plight? Why is it that they created a space around themselves which left no way out of this plight, no way around it or through it?

One can begin with the incredible career of Theodore Herzl, the founder of the Zionist movement which attempted, beginning in the last decade of the nineteenth century, to establish a national home for the Jews of the world. Herzl, himself an assimilated Jew from Vienna, was of the opinion that his people could never be accepted or assimilated by Gentile society since they tended to encapsulate themselves within the confines of their own culture, traditions, and religion. The only way the Jews could find an expression of their Jewish consciousness, could escape persecution and rejuvenate their heritage, was by the creation of an exclusive homeland where Jewish men and women could live in peace, no longer vulnerable to Gentile hostility. There was no better place, surely, for the "ingathering of the exiles" than Palestine, Eretz Israel, the ancient homeland from which the Jews themselves had been expelled two thousand years before.

In 1896, Herzl wrote *A Jewish State*, an idealized account of this political dream, in which he expounded his concept of Zionism, a concept concerned with the notion of "transporting a people without a country to a country without a people." It is interesting to note that nowhere in his book did the author mention the indigenous population already in Palestine. He was either ignorant of its existence or, in an age that condoned the ceding of other people's territory and the imposition of a European culture, seen as being to their betterment, he did not feel their fate warranted consideration. Herzl was satisfied to assure the world that "we should there form a portion of the rampart of Europe against Asia, an outpost of civilization as opposed to barbarism." °

A year later a Zionist Congress was held. Zionist leaders built support for their movement; their voice was heard and their gospel understood. Their efforts culminated in 1917 when the British government, which was to be granted mandate rule over Palestine

---

° *A Jewish State* (London, 1896), p. 29.

after World War I, gave concrete hopes to Zionist aspirations by declaring that it viewed with favor the creation of a national Jewish Home in Palestine, and issued what came to be known as the Balfour Declaration. Among other things, this stated that the rights of the people already living there were not to be subordinated as a result of, nor was the Jewish Home to be established at the cost of, the dispossession of the Palestinians:

> His Majesty's Government view with favour the establishment in Palestine of a national home for the Jewish people, and will use their best endeavours to facilitate the achievement of this object, it being clearly understood that nothing shall be done to prejudice the civil and religious rights of existing non-Jewish communities in Palestine.

But the Palestinians on whose soil another national state was to be superimposed, whose destiny was consequently to undergo a devastating change, were never consulted.° In Palestine the initial response to Jewish immigration, particularly prior to the Balfour Declaration, was one of indifference; the Arab world had in the past accepted settlement on its territory by foreign peoples who wished to preserve their old language, culture, and traditions. This was so especially in the case of the Armenians in the Middle East. However, when it became clear that the newly arrived Europeans were the vanguard of a people that harbored intentions of being not just foreign settlers, but foreign occupiers, the Zionists came face to face with spontaneous hostility from both the local population and the Arab world in general. Jewish immigrants nevertheless continued to arrive in Palestine in very large numbers, although they still formed a small percentage of the population.

° In negotiations with Lord Lansdowne, representative of the British government, the Zionists were initially asked to consider Kenya. As in the case of Palestine, there is no record that an inquiry into the wishes of the "natives" preceded the offer. In an interview (*The Observer* [London], January 17, 1971) at her home, Golda Meir made the most ironic statement of her career: "Some Zionists were prepared to have a Jewish homeland in, say, Africa—like Uganda," she said. "I was opposed to that. Sometimes when I have been in Africa in the last few years, I have said to myself: 'My God! And to think we might have been here! And what would the independent countries of Africa be doing about that today!' "

To the Zionists, to the Mandate government, and to the world, the million Palestinians who had been living in their ancient homeland for centuries were merely wretched natives and not sensitive human beings whose fate in history was about to be affected. It may astonish a lot of people when I say they *were* human beings who felt pain when they suffered, laughed when they were happy, and dreamed when they contemplated the future. There were peasants working on the land, there were shopkeepers tending their merchandise, there were teachers and students in their schools, there were housewives in their homes, there were men working on their goals. There were towns throbbing, houses building, mosques and churches being visited. There were thieves and vagabonds and lunatics, and there were poets and scholars and singers. And because I want to indulge in a return in my mind to the time when I was a child, I will add that there was a small township, near Haifa, which had a square in the middle of it where the locals gathered at evening time to play backgammon, dance the dabke, and listen to the oud. This was real to me, to us, and its intensity and poignance were not, and are not, negated by those who, thousands of miles away, smug in their seats of power, denied my existence over my pleas, and decided my fate over my head.

After World War II and the tragedy of the concentration camps, world conscience and world support surrendered to Zionism at any cost. The breath of Zionist afflatus became strong in its immediacy. Despite attempts by the Mandate authorities to appease the alarmed Palestinians by stemming the flow of Jewish immigrants into Palestine, thousands still poured in. Jewish political leaders, backed by armed and militant terrorist organizations, were not prepared to hide or sugar-coat the fact that they intended to build a Jewish nation on the land of Palestine.

The history of Palestine between the Mandate and the withdrawal of the British is a chronicle of anarchy, claims and counter-claims, death and destruction, raids and reprisals between the two communities, while the British authorities stood helplessly by, unable to impose or interest the parties in a compromise solution. The Palestinians would not accept the partition of their homeland; nor were the Jews, still a minority, willing to live merely as

citizens of Palestine. On April 19, 1936, Arab riots broke out in
Jaffa which resulted in the imposition of a curfew and the enforce-
ment of emergency regulations. This prompted Palestinian leaders
to call for a general strike and, a few days later, to form the
Higher Arab Committee to coordinate political and resistance activities. (The Committee was later outlawed and its leaders sent
into exile.) This date may be taken to mark the beginning of the
disturbances that continued up to 1948. It presaged the ominous
future awaiting the Arabs and Zionists. The impasse was never resolved, despite various commissions, sponsored first by the British
government, then by the United Nations, that attempted to investigate the possibility of an answer acceptable to both groups.

Shortly before the end of 1947, the UN passed a resolution par-
titioning Palestine into a Jewish state and a Palestinian state, with
Jerusalem an international city bound to both states by an economic union. But the UN, helpless to put the plan into practice,
and the British, unwilling to shoulder the burden of implementing
it, left the two communities to solve their own problems as best
they could. British troops were evacuated on May 15, 1948.

The conflict between the Zionists and the Palestinians, which
took on the character of a Greek tragedy as each step followed
predictably on the heels of the preceding one, was renewed and
intensified. Palestine became a country facing violence and rehearsing for a showdown. The Irgun and the Hagana, two formi-
dable and ruthless Zionist organizations, commenced a campaign
of terror against isolated towns and villages. Their purpose was to
frighten as many Palestinians as possible into fleeing the country,
thereby insuring a homogeneous Israel. In one operation alone, on
April 9, 1948, a detachment of the Irgun attacked the small rural
community of Deir Yassin and killed every man, woman, and
child of its 254 inhabitants. Although the Hagana was not equally
savage, its modus operandi was designed to achieve the same end:
to precipitate a mass exodus of Palestinians out of the country. In
his book, *The Revolt—Story of the Irgun*, Menachem Begin,
leader of the terrorist organization, gloats over the massacre thus:
"The legend of Deir Yassin helped us in particular in the saving of
Tiberias and the conquest of Haifa. . . . All the Jewish forces pro-

ceeded to advance through Haifa like a knife through butter. The Arabs began fleeing in panic, shouting Deir Yassin. . . . Arabs throughout the country were seized by limitless panic and started to flee for their lives." °

The Hagana's efforts in that direction are described by Arthur Koestler, who was witness to them in the final months of 1948. "By that time," he says, "Hagana was using not only its radio station but also loudspeaker vans which blared their sinister news from the vicinity of the Arab sooks. They warned the Arab population to keep clear of the billets of the foreign mercenaries who had infiltrated into town, warned them to send their women and children away before the new contingent of savage Irakis arrived, promised them safe conducts and escorts to Arab territory, and hinted at terrible consequences if their warnings were disregarded." †

The Israelis were immensely successful in their aim of creating a state "clean of Arabs." For a people like the Palestinians, without arms or leadership, a people long subdued by the Turks and the British and pitted against an enemy unwilling to elevate itself above the perpetration of massacres, there was no choice but flight. In later years the story of this flight, as understood in the West and as told by Zionist propagandists, had it that the million or so refugees who poured into Syria, Lebanon, and Jordan "were urged to do so by the Arab governments" whose armies were mobilizing to attack the soon-to-be-declared state of Israel. This has since been exposed as a myth. An examination of radio monitoring records in the West revealed no such appeals to the population of Palestine from the neighboring states; rather, it was revealed that the Palestinians were exhorted *not to leave their homeland.*‡

° *The Revolt—Story of the Irgun* (New York: Henry Schuman, Inc., 1951).

† *Promise and Fulfillment: Palestine 1917–1949* (New York: Macmillan, 1949).

‡ The reader is referred to an article in the London *Spectator* of May 12, 1961, by Erskine Childers, which confirms this and gives an account of the exodus of the refugees. In a balanced statement in his book *Cross Roads to Israel* (Cleveland: World Publishing Co., 1965), Christopher Sykes writes: "It can be said with a high degree of certainty that . . . if the exodus was by and large an accident of war in the first stage, in the latter stages it was consciously and mercilessly helped on by Jewish threats and aggression toward the Arab population."

Soon after the dispersion of these people was accomplished their immense lands and their properties were immediately seized by Zionist agencies which declared their owners "absentees." *
This action, which was sanctioned by all the Zionist political parties, including the left, and initiated by the government itself, was not restricted to absentees, but, by virtue of a hastily introduced series of laws, was extended to "present absentees." This category included Palestinians who were very much present as citizens of Israel but who happened to be absent from their towns, villages, or farms on a certain date. Thus a Palestinian farmer who had gone to the next village to escape the fighting would return home to find himself classified as an "absentee." In most cases whole families, bereft of the land to which they and their family system had been rooted for centuries, would hire themselves out at settlements and work as hired hands on their own lands.

Dr. Don Peretz, in his book *Israel and the Palestine Arabs*, tries to untangle the complicated legalisms of this land robbery which came to be known as the Absentee Property Law. He estimates that 300,000 dunams† were taken away from Israeli Palestinians in this manner and that 4,000,000 additional dunams of land left behind by the refugees were confiscated by the authorities. He calculates that the export of fruit from formerly Arab land accounted for 10 percent of Israel's foreign currency earnings in 1951, and that the country's third largest export was provided by olive groves, 95 percent of which had belonged to Palestinians.‡

In an earlier study that appeared in 1954 he wrote that:

Nearly half the new Jewish immigrants live in homes abandoned by the Arabs. They occupy nearly 400 Arab towns and villages. About a quarter of the buildings now in use in Israel formerly were Arab

---

* Official UNRWA estimates confirm the figure of 726,000 originally made by the United Nations Survey Mission. This figure does not take into account those thousands of refugees who, for one reason or another, did not register with UNRWA.

† A dunam is one-quarter of an acre.

‡ *Israel and the Palestine Arabs*, foreword by Roger Baldwin (Washington: The Middle East Institute, 1958).

property. The Arabs left over 10,000 shops and stores in Jewish hands. The Israel Custodian of Absentee Property took over more than 4,000,000 dunams of former Arab land, or nearly 60 percent of the country's cultivable area. This was nearly two and a half times the total Jewish-owned property at the time the state of Israel was established, and includes most of its olive orchards, a large part of its fruit and vegetable crop land and almost half the citrus groves.*

In January 1954 the Israeli daily *Ha'aretz* published a series of articles by Moshe Karen to protest the government action taken against "a helpless minority." The author stated that

here was a case of wholesale robbery in legal guise. Hundreds of thousands of dunams of land were taken away from the Arab minority—I am not talking here of the refugees—through a whole variety of legal devices. . . . Even more depressing is the fact that it was those same groups who presume to establish a new society free from injustice and exploitation—the kibbutzim, in other words—who marched in the vanguard of the seizure campaign.

Those Palestinians who did stay behind, roughly 12 percent of the original population, people who neither took up arms against Israel nor aided the Arab armies in 1948, were placed under military control and treated as an inferior people. They were reduced to second-class citizenship status and discriminated against on every level. Occasional acts of violence against them did not stop with the cessation of hostilities in 1948 but continued up to 1967, when they acquired a more sinister and horrifying nature.

In the June 13, 1967, issue of the *Christian Science Monitor*, we are informed that

Israeli security forces have on occasion dealt ruthlessly with Arabs more recently than 1948. Two incidents in particular are remembered fearfully by the Arabs. The first was in the Jordanian village of Qibya in October 1953, when Israeli regular soldiers killed 53 men, women, and children in retaliation for the killing of an Israeli mother and her two children, apparently by a saboteur from Jordan. The second was at Kafr Qassem, an Arab village within Israel, in October

---

* See "The Arab Refugee Dilemma," *Foreign Affairs* (October 1954), pp. 137–38.

1956, during the 100-hour Sinai war of that year. Israeli border police shot and killed 51 Israeli Arabs, including women and children, who were returning from the fields at the end of the day's work and were unwittingly in breach of a curfew order.*

John Cogley, the respected editor of *Commonweal*, a Catholic liberal periodical published in the United States, reported on a visit he made to Israel in 1954. A group of Israeli Palestinians had been waiting for two years to return home to Ikrit, a Catholic village, and in despair took their case to court, winning a ruling in their favor: "Before they could move back to their homes, Israeli planes dropped bombs on their abandoned town, destroying everything. Whether from malice or not no one can say, but the date chosen for this wholly Christian village was December 25th. . . . [Last September] Kafr Biram, another Catholic village, was destroyed. . . . In both cases, the reason offered for the destruction of the Catholic villages was 'military security.' " †

Palestinian intellectuals, writers, and poets were the group probably most discriminated against. The notorious preventive detention law permits the imprisonment, without the mercy of a time limit, of any person whose incarceration is considered "necessary or expedient . . . for securing the public safety, . . . the maintenance of public order, or the suppression of mutiny, rebellion, or riot." Whatever this law purports to prevent, and for whatever reasons it is deemed expedient, it is still a law that permits the indefinite detention of persons who have not been tried or convicted.

The great irony that can never be detached from this law is its origin: it was initially promulgated by the Mandate government in 1937 as the Emergency Defense Regulations and directed at Zionist terrorism. During that time the Federation of Hebrew Lawyers met to "abolish the emergency regulations and restore the elementary rights to the individual." Dr. Alan M. Dershowitz, profes-

---

* For a detailed and documented account of this massacre, see Hal Draper in *Zionism, Israel, and the Arabs: The Historical Background to the Middle East Tragedy*, Walter Laqueur, ed. (Berkeley, 1967).

† "Majority and Minorities," *Commonweal*, January 22, 1954, p. 401.

sor of law at Harvard University, visited Israel in the autumn of 1970 to report on the preventive detention law and noted: "When Israel was established as a state, the emergency regulations—including preventive detention—remained on the books, to be used sporadically until the Six-Day War of 1967 and more extensively after Israel's victory and the resulting occupation."

Dr. Dershowitz discusses the case of Fawzi el-Asmar, a poet and Israeli Arab, in the December 1970 issue of *Commentary*.* Fawzi, he reported, "used to write his poems at home in Lydda near the Tel Aviv International Airport. Now he writes them in Damon Prison . . . Fawzi is one of twenty-three Israeli Arabs being held in preventive detention by the Israeli military authorities." Dr. Dershowitz gives an account of his meeting with Fawzi at Damon Prison. "I walked among the inmates and asked for Fawzi. A tall man emerged, strikingly handsome with a captivating smile. Looking more mature than his thirty-one years, Fawzi emitted an aura of confidence, determination, and honesty. I could tell . . . that Fawzi el-Asmar is a leader of men."

The poet was asked why he was being detained, and his reply was: "Because I am an Arab." The interviewer explained that there were 300,000 Israeli Arabs and not all were in preventive detention. Why was he chosen? "Because," Dr. Dershowitz tells us Fawzi replied, "I express the feelings of the 300,000 and that makes me dangerous. There are Jews who share my beliefs, maybe even some who express them better. But they are not dangerous because they are Jews . . . That is why I am being detained, and not Meir Vilner." † What reason was given by the security police for his detention? The authorities concocted a story about his connection with the guerrillas, he said, and about being a terrorist organizer. "Were you a terrorist organizer?" the professor asked. "If they could have proved it, they would have brought me to trial."

Sabri Jiryis, a brilliant 31-year-old Palestinian lawyer, was im-

* "Terrorism and Preventive Detention: The Case of Israel," *Commentary* (December 1970), pp. 67 f.

† The Jewish head of Rakah, the Arab Communist Party that advocates a binational state and the dismantling of Zionist exclusivism.

prisoned by the authorities, also under preventive detention, for publishing a book titled *The Arabs in Israel*, which was later confiscated by the government.° Jiryis, who practiced law in Haifa, was no stranger to preventive detention or Damon Prison for he began writing and speaking against the government as a teenage student at Hebrew University and was one of the founders of Al-Ard, an activist movement of Palestinian students. Since 1955, he had lived with a police order limiting his movements to the city of Haifa, which restricted his personal and professional life. On June 8, 1967, Jiryis was arrested, along with a handful of other Palestinian intellectuals, for "security purposes." On February 20, 1970, he was again detained at Damon Prison where he stayed for three months. His release was secured after the case received modest international attention and Jiryis's French publisher, accompanied by a continental lawyer, arrived in Jerusalem. The Palestinian lawyer's most recent detention, according to Professor Dershowitz, who succeeded in interviewing him as well as Fawzi el-Asmar and many others, resulted from information the Shin Bet (the Israeli secret police) had, that a Lebanese individual, caught illegally trying to cross the border, had "mentioned his name." They claimed that his brother Jarius once crossed the border into Lebanon to join Al-Fatah and that he had "harbored him on his way to carrying out a terrorist mission." He was put in prison "to prevent him from carrying out further collaborative work with his terrorist brother, who was still at large."

"They detained me because of my political views," Jiryis told Dr. Dershowitz. The case against Sabri Jiryis, he writes, "was the least convincing of the many cases I had investigated."

Another victim of preventive detention was Mahmoud Dar-

° A copy found its way to the outside world and was later translated into English. Reviewing the book, which was documented from Hebrew sources, the *Manchester Guardian* (December 12, 1968) said: "A scholarly work, it is a forthright and comprehensive study of the Arab minority in Israel. It contains the fullest and most vivid account yet published of the notorious Kafr Qassem affair in which Israeli soldiers systematically killed 49 [sic] Arab villagers as they returned home in ignorance of a curfew which had been imposed at short notice." A revised edition of the book will soon be published by Monthly Review Press.

weesh, the poet, who was continually being moved in and out of
jail for offending Israeli sensibilities. In 1964, his poem "Investiga-
tion" was deemed subversive and he was returned to jail. The
poem said in part:

> Write down I am an Arab,
> my card number is 50,000
> I have eight children
> the ninth will come next summer.
> Are you angry?
>
> Write down I am an Arab,
> I cut stone with comrade laborers,
> I squeeze the rock
> to get a loaf,
> to get a book
> for my eight children.
> But I do not plead charity
> and I do not cringe
> under your rule.
> Are you angry?
>
> Write down I am an Arab,
> I am a name without a title,
> steadfast in a frenzied world.
>
> My roots sink deep
> beyond the ages,
> beyond time.
>
> I am the son of the plough,
> of humble peasant stock.
> I live in a hut
> of reed and stalk.
> The hair: jet black.
> The eyes: brown.
> My Arab headdress
> scratches intruding hands,
> and I prefer a dip of oil and thyme.
>
> And please write down,
> on top of all,

I hate nobody,
I rob nobody,
but when I starve
I eat the flesh of my marauders.
Beware,
beware my hunger,
beware my wrath.

There were some elements in Israel who were agitating for even more restrictions on the Palestinians. In a heated debate on the Citizenship Law in the Knesset in 1950, Moshe Shapiro, then Minister of the Interior, chastised the government for granting "automatic Israeli citizenship to 63,000 foreigners who were registered on November 30, 1948."

Foreigners!

A bitter account of how these "foreigners" are made to feel about their foreignness may be found in "Le Conflit israelo-arabe," a special issue of *Les Temps Modernes* which was being issued as the Six Day War broke out. A contributor to this symposium was an Israeli Palestinian, Ibrahim Shabath, who taught Hebrew in Arab schools and was editor-in-chief of *Al-Mirsad*, an Arabic daily. His contribution, along with those of other Israeli Palestinians, was presented anonymously for fear of the authorities. Mr. Shabath complained that Palestinians were considered strangers and aliens in their own country and persecuted mercilessly. In a conversation that he once had with David ben Gurion, he was told: "You must know that Israel is the country of the Jews and only of the Jews. Every Arab who lives here has the same rights as any minority citizen in any other country of the world, but he must admit the fact that he lives in a Jewish country."

"It is not without reason that they [Israeli Arabs] have been called the 'niggers of Israel,' " says Hal Draper. "But as a matter of fact, the American Negroes would not have taken lying down what the Israeli Arabs had to endure for two decades." °

The defeat the Arab armies suffered in the first Arab-Israeli war in 1948 left the Arab world inchoate and stunned, and precipi-

---

° "The Origins of the Middle East Crisis," in *The Israel-Arab Reader*, Walter Laqueur, ed. (London: Pelican Books, 1970).

tated innumerable upheavals in its regimes. King Abdulla of Jordan was assassinated as he went into Al-Aqsa mosque in Jerusalem; Syria was shaken by a series of coups d'etat; the prime minister of Lebanon was shot dead as he was being driven through the streets of Amman on a state visit; King Farouk was overthrown and a military junta, headed by Colonel Nasser, ruled over Egypt and abolished the monarchy; and the Iraqi royal family, along with the hated Nuri el-Said, were murdered in the streets of Baghdad.

This period also marked a new phase in the misfortunes of the Palestinian people, most of whom found themselves, as the first decade of the fifties opened, concentrated in refugee camps in Lebanon, Syria, and Jordan. The Israelis became well entrenched in a Jewish state (occupying far larger areas, through military conquest, than even the original UN partition plan allotted them); the eastern part of Palestine was annexed by Jordan, which henceforth alluded to it as the West Bank; and the southern strip of Gaza was occupied by the Egyptian military authorities (who proceeded to treat the people worse than their Israeli counterparts did across the border).

The nation of Palestine ceased to be. Its original inhabitants, the Palestinian people, were dubbed Arab refugees, sent regular food rations by the UN, and forgotten by the world.

Some of the readers of this book may be among those who idealize "the miracle in the desert," admire Israeli accomplishments, romanticize its "kibbutzim, the watch on the frontier, and suntanned sabras," and read partisan versions of its creation; they may find it difficult to admit that beneath the glamor lies the tragedy of another people who suffered for no reason, who were uprooted from their homeland, and who had never in their history practiced persecution in their rencontre with Jews, but who were made to pay the price of a crime that others had committed. In order to allow the realization of the Zionist political dream and solve the Jewish refugee problem, the world felt no qualms in hastening our diaspora, then forgetting our existence, our yearning, and our pain.

The period beginning in 1948 and stretching for two decades sees the addition of a newer dimension of destitution to the lives of the Palestinian people. Unable to accept the *fait accompli* of Israel and the incomprehensible notion that they may never return home, they persisted in clinging to the hope that soon the conscience of the world would come to their aid. Was it not Judaized by the plight of the Jewish refugees? Will it not be equally Palestinianized by our own plight?

But if world conscience was concerned, it was merely for the fate and welfare of "tiny Israel." The Israelis, unwilling to put themselves in a double bind by conceding the rights of the refugees, declared that there were no such people in existence. "Arab refugees" were to be absorbed in Arab countries. The homelessness and alienation that are a recurring theme in Jewish history become stunningly ironic when viewed in this context.

This left the Arabs as the only potential saviors. But the world of the Arabs, gripped by one crisis after another, was itself in search of a hero, a man with charisma and a vision of their destiny; a leader to fill the vacuum that existed in the wake of their military defeat; an ideologue and a political thinker to rally the masses and work toward the fulfillment of their dreams. The absence of such a leader enabled Nasser, the one-eyed man, to become king.

Although Egypt itself had hitherto never been, geographically, culturally, or ethnically, part of the Levantine, the Arab world proper, Nasser proceeded to adopt policies of direct activism in Arab affairs and pan-Arabism. His initial emergence on the scene did indeed rally behind him the nascent working and middle classes, who believed his grandiose promises to "drive the Jews into the sea," obliterate the last vestige of imperialism from the area, unite all "Arab" lands and topple all the reactionary regimes.

In less than two years, the Egyptian president became a near legendary figure whose verbal pyrotechnics enhanced his image with the Arabs, who placed around his head a halo never worn by any of their leaders before Saladin. His prestige was progressively improved following the successful negotiations that led to the evacuation of British troops from Egypt and the nationalization of the Canal. His survival after the Suez crisis of 1956 and his emergence as a "victor" against the combined aggression of Israeli,

British, and French forces, left no doubt in the minds of the Arab masses as to whom they would turn in their moment of crisis and for their moment of glory.

The hour of triumph was indeed at hand, they were told. Unite Arabs! the speakers of Radio Cairo shrieked, for soon the Americans and their Israeli lackeys will be trampled by the boots of your victorious armies. Unite, they were told, unite, for soon the Americans who amputated a piece of your homeland and usurped your Palestine will learn their lesson. "Here we shall bury American international gangsterism and its Zionist agents," Radio Cairo claimed. "Arabs dig graves everywhere, dig them for every American presence. Dig up all the homeland. Dig up all the homeland. Dig it Arabs. Dig it Arabs. Dig it Arabs. Dig it Arabs. Dig it Arabs."

On February 1, 1958, the United Arab Republic was proclaimed, to the jubilation of the masses who viewed it as a prelude to total unity of all Arabs. But soon after the union was effected, the Egyptians proceeded to act as ruthless occupiers, with the Syrians subordinated on every level. Political parties were banned, labor unions were virtually under police control, the economic and social structure was undermined, and Syrians from all walks of life were jailed for opposing the Egyptian bureaucrats and Egyptian army officers who had swarmed to the "Northern Province."

Within three years the "Northerners," chafing from Egyptian exploitation of their economy and the arrogance of the "Southerners" who had grafted themselves on their society, had had enough. On September 28, 1961, they seceded from the UAR, deported the pro-consul and his fellow Egyptians from the area and, as it were, slapped Nasser in the face. This marked the turning of the tide in the political fortunes of the Egyptian leader.

At this stage Nasser did in effect withdraw from the affairs of the Levant; but he continued his intransigence and expanded his propaganda media, which he used to denounce Saudi Arabia, Syria, and Tunisia. He broke off relations with Jordan. He refused to recognize the new Syrian regime and generally antagonized other Arab heads of state—but still talked of Arab unity and his avowed aim of driving the Jews into the sea. Israel had in the meantime become a viable state that was militarily capable of holding its own against the combined but uncoordinated forces of the Arab armies. Although the Israelis wanted peace, they wanted it on their own terms, rejecting attempts by President Kennedy, for one, to pressure them into allowing the repatriation of *some* refugees as an initial goodwill gesture. They wanted a settlement that included recognition by the Arab states of the Israeli status quo as the Israelis saw it: an Israel that was "as Jewish as England was English." ° They rigidly claimed that the refugees from Palestine had fled "voluntarily" and had consequently forfeited their right to repatriation. They rejected international law (and several UN resolutions), which said that whether a refugee left his homeland voluntarily or was encouraged to do so, he had the right to return, for all wars create refugees who go back to take up their lives again when the armies have departed and the guns become silent. But the Israelis remained adamant, although throughout the 1950's they intensified their efforts to fulfill the main task of their Zionist movement by enticing Jews from all countries of the world to settle in the Jewish state, and David ben Gurion, on an arm-twisting visit to the United States in 1954, denounced the Zionist Organization of America for not working toward moving the entire Jewish population of America to Israel.

° The original statement ("Palestine will ultimately become as Jewish as England is English") was made by Chaim Weizmann at the Paris Peace Conference on February 23, 1919, and is quoted in his autobiography *Trial and Error* (New York: Harper & Brothers, 1949), p. 244. Dayan said the same thing slightly differently when he appeared on CBS's *Face the Nation* on June 11, 1967. He was asked by Sidney Grusen of the *New York Times* if Israel could absorb the people whose territory it had just occupied in the June War:

Dayan: Economically we can; but I think that is not in accord with our aims in the future. It would turn Israel into either a binational or poly-Arab-Jewish state, and we want a Jewish state. We can absorb them but then it won't be the same country.

Grusen: And it is necessary in your opinion to maintain this as a Jewish state and a purely Jewish state?

Dayan: Absolutely, absolutely. We want a Jewish state like the French have a French state.

Nasser, not normally endowed with great political wisdom, did in fact recognize the reality of Israel and its determination to endure in the region—but he refused to say so publicly. His policy was to lie low but to continue his threats to annihilate what the world still termed "tiny Israel."

Even the most pro-Western of Arab statesmen, and those most resigned to the concept of Israel in the Middle East, could not have risked a public stance of rapprochement with Jerusalem. President Bourguiba of Tunisia brought the wrath of the Arab world on him when he suggested in a speech on April 21, 1965, that a saner policy be adopted by the Arabs in their dispute with Israel. He proposed that the Arabs recognize the Israeli *fait accompli* and seek peace; Israel in return would withdraw to the borders allotted it by the UN resolution in 1947, and, though ceding a bit of territory, would gain peace. His offer was totally rejected by the Israelis, and the Arabs were aghast at the gruesome spectacle of a leader publicly advocating rapprochement with the Zionists. His government was condemned at the Arab League, demonstrators in Cairo, Beirut, and Damascus denounced him, a street named after him in Amman was quickly renamed, and he was generally taken to task by the press. On April 23, Cairo's semi-official daily, *Al-Ahram*, responded thus: "He was moving according to a plan coordinated by the forces of Western imperialism." *Al-Akhbar* said: "Bourguiba has stabbed the Arab people in the back."

The Tunisian president's reaction to all this was indignation, for he claimed that in private conversations he had held with Nasser, the Egyptian leader had revealed to him that he had had no plans for attacking Israel, or restoring Palestine to the refugees, and wished to see peace reign in the Middle East.

No Arab leader before or after Bourguiba dared endanger his position or add fuel to the unrest of the masses by following in his footsteps. But they knew that Israel, although a Western diktat implanted in their midst by the colonial past, was now beyond the juncture in their history when it could be dislodged. The most naive politician realized that even in the most unlikely event that the Arabs became better armed, and in the unlikelier event that they became more effective behind their guns than their counterparts in Israel, the Western world was not sufficiently indifferent to allow the driving of two million Jews into the sea; and Russia, though anxious for a foothold in the Middle East, would not risk a confrontation with the Americans by fighting alongside the Arabs to destroy Israel.

So in the early 1960's, the Arab countries, still stubborn about "usurped Palestine," nevertheless turned to other more immediate problems. Nasser was engaged in his propaganda war against the "lackeys of imperialism" and concurrently concentrating on improving Egypt's economy and the plight of the fellah (still living and working under medieval conditions). In the Arabian Peninsula, the patriarchal monarchs of Saudi Arabia and the Persian Gulf protectorates were receiving immense fortunes in oil revenues and insuring that their hapless masses did not acquire too many radical ideas, too much education, or too great a voice in deciding their future.

At the same time, the Arab world was in disarray and divided. The Baath Party in Iraq had overthrown Quassem's regime and killed off 5,000 of its sympathizers; Nasser was engaged in a miniwar against the Yemeni Royalists, following his decision to intervene militarily on the side of Sallal, the army officer who had overthrown the Immam; Syria was antagonistic toward Lebanon; relations between Iraq and Egypt were strained; Saudi Arabia was virtually at war with Egypt over Yemen; the Maghreb countries were engaged in disputes over Mauritania and with each other; and in the Levant, rivalries polarized Iraqi and Syrian Baathists, Maronite and Lebanese irredentists, and Hashemite royalists and Arab nationalists.

We return to the Palestinians, whom we now find, in the early stages of their expulsion from Palestine, considering no solution to their problem other than the return to their homeland, and opting to suffer in DP camps for what they think is the duration of a few months, a few years, rather than accept integration and national oblivion.

As time went on, the social life of the refugee family, whose members lived in crowded ghettos or leaky tents, was being changed cataclysmically. The refugee, who in Palestine had been a middle-class urban dweller, tradesman, or farmer, now found his individuality, self-reliance, and initiative smothered, and, most crucially, his value structure and family system disintegrating under the pressures of an increasingly oppressive and futile existence.

International efforts on behalf of the refugees sought at first to find a long-term political solution. The United Nations Palestine Mediator, Count Folke Bernadotte (who was later assassinated by Israeli terrorists), spent much time working on the obvious solution to the problem, which was repatriation. His recommendations ultimately found their way into a UN resolution vainly calling on the Israelis to allow the return of the Palestinians to their homeland. Behind the scenes, the British and particularly the Americans were anxious to see a settlement projected according to the concept of compensation-integration, and helped in the establishment of the Conciliation Commission of Palestine (CCP) which was called upon "to overcome economic dislocations created by the hostilities . . . [and] to reintegrate the refugees into the economic life of the area." Major schemes for the resettlement of refugees and their integration in, and possibly outside, their host countries were proposed and a large capital outlay for that purpose was set up. All this was rejected by the Palestinians. Then the CCP, fathering another committee by creating the Economic Survey Mission, opted to escape opposition by proposing works projects, such as road construction, housing, and irrigation, that would find productive employment for the refugees. The UN General Assembly authorized the Mission to spend, through UNRWA, $250.7 million to see its recommendations come to fruition.

The refugees viewed these suspicious machinations as attempts by foreigners to prejudice their rights to repatriation and as a result lent them little cooperation. Frequent manifestos were issued by refugee organizations which condemned the Mission for submitting plans to resettle or integrate them, thus robbing them of their right to a return to Palestine. Instead of stating the terms under which this plan was to be undertaken, and giving unequivocal assurances to the Palestinians that the public works projects did not aim at subjecting them to ultimate oblivion in their host countries, the director of UNRWA made a round of the Arab capitals to explain his plans; he preferred parleys with various committees of the Arab League to discussions with Palestinian representatives.

The project, which was to be a three-year program, was a great and costly failure. Of the 878,000 refugees registered with UNRWA, the largest number ever employed was just over 12,000 and seven months later it had dwindled to 812. In the end, the only groups that benefited were the local governments. In its report to the General Assembly, UNRWA stated that it had "found itself financing and operating labor camps to build public works" from which only the host countries derived any advantage. Before the Mission was dissolved, its chairman, Gordon R. Clapp, advised that "the region is not ready, the projects are not ready, the people and governments are not ready . . ."

Exit Mission. Enter Reintegration Fund, November 1950 ($30 million). The purpose was to set aside funds to reintegrate those refugees who chose such a course or to help in small projects that aided in the settlement of enterprising Palestinians outside the camps. Egypt drew on the fund for a survey of the Sinai Desert, and Jordan used it with no discernible profit for the refugees.

What the General Assembly and its various "Arab refugee" commissions did not at any stage become aware of was the nature of the drama being played in the minds of the Palestinian people regarding their homeland, and the reluctance the Arab states themselves had for absorbing over one million refugees in their midst. It would have been impossible for Egypt to integrate in its overpopulated Nile valley or in its economically depressed society the 200,000 Palestinians under Egyptian military rule, then virtually locked up in the Gaza Strip. Egypt's own educated elite was encouraged by the government to emigrate to other Arab countries. Thus the Gaza refugees, even in the event that they agreed to and were accepted for integration, were doomed to the

Strip area—barred from entering Egypt to the south, returning to their homeland to the north, or, by Israeli fire, from reaching the Arab states to the east.

Syria, which could have absorbed its own refugees, and probably those in Lebanon and Jordan, was continually shaken by coups d'etat, was slow in developing its resources for its own people, and generally struggled with a budget showing a chronic deficit. Conditions for a constructive settlement program under an unstable and militarily oriented regime were not favorable.

Resettlement of the refugees in Lebanon, under any designation or at any juncture in time, was never a question. Lebanon, with a delicate and at times precarious communal, religious, and social balance in its population, was hostile to the idea of welcoming as citizens any Palestinians whose loyalties were considered dubious and whose numbers might overturn the structure of the legislative branches (membership in which was said to be proportional to, and representative of, the various religious sects in the country).

The Jordanian case was unique in this context, for although the Palestinians formed over half the population, the majority of them lived in the West Bank, originally part of Palestine. Thus a great number were refugees in their own country—refugees who had fled en masse from areas that were allotted to or captured by the Israelis. Jordan had the highest concentration of Palestinians but, with its barren East Bank and rocky arid hillsides, had also traditionally been the most underdeveloped part of the Levant. Any large-scale resettlement programs would therefore have been doomed to failure.

These considerations, however, were at all times merely academic, for in their pronouncements the Arab governments continued to oppose schemes for integration on the grounds that these would be tantamount to admission of defeat by Israel; would be what the Zionists themselves wanted; and would facilitate imperialist manipulation of the Arab world. All this was true, but the price for this intransigence and inflexibility was paid by the Palestinians alone and not by the Arabs. The enervating and degrading existence led by the Palestinians was, and remains, of no concern to those who spoke on their behalf. Pawn politics and indifference were the two foci of a problem of tragic and human dimensions.

At this stage the United Nations and its agency, UNRWA, gave up on any further attempts to mediate, integrate, or alleviate, and restricted their activities to a regular issuance of food rations to the refugees. In the meantime, those Palestinians in Jordan who were living in border villages and small towns or huddled in camps or caves, and who could thus see their own farms, houses, or gardens across the hills being settled by Israeli immigrants, started crossing the armistice line to "go home." A great many of these simple folk, to whom politics, war, and frontiers were an alien concept, had the naive notion that once the hostilities ceased they could return home to resume their lives, to meet the members of their families they had left behind, to sleep in their warm houses, and to be in their orange groves—for soon it would be the orange-picking season.

"These Arabs returning to look for their homes were at first almost entirely unarmed," says Lieutenant General J. B. Glubb, in an article written for *Foreign Affairs* magazine at the time. "A great number of them were shot dead, without question or answer, by the first Israeli patrol they met. Others were maltreated or tortured." ° These people, whom the Israelis called "infiltrators," did not come only from the Jordan border areas but also from the Gaza Strip. Some of them had been merchants who had for centuries conducted their business with Lebanon, Syria, and Jordan; they continued to cross Beersheba with their pack animals carrying rice, sugar, and other goods to the other side. Others crossed Gaza to go into Jordan to look for work, to search for relatives, or to engage in legitimate trade. "None of these persons who crossed the Beersheba area wished to attack the Jews," continues Glubb. "But Israeli patrols frequently intercepted and killed them. And as the numbers of killed increased, so did the numbers of embittered persons mount up. Men whose fathers, brothers, sons or even wives and daughters had been killed on the Gaza car-

---

° "Violence on the Jordan-Israel Border: A Jordanian View," *Foreign Affairs* (July 1954), p. 556.

avans longed for revenge." Some of them returned, and this time they were fully armed and the first to shoot.

Israeli violence against "infiltrators" did not stop at intercept-shoot-and-kill but was extended to reprisal raids on those villages or locales from which men crossed the border. This resulted in death to men, women, and children and destruction to property and homes, as platoon attacks from Israel became the order of the day. The Israelis had gone to great pains to kick these people out in 1948 and they were not having them back now.

The most basic change that was to occur among the Palestinian people would be the emergence of a new generation which, although as fiercely attached to Palestine as its elders, was less bitter and self-destructive in the way it viewed the problem. It accepted, when it did not seek, opportunities for rehabilitation, assistance, vocational training, scholarships, and the chance for a normal life. But the social structure of the Palestinian family, whose atmosphere engendered a deep and constant hope for the return to Palestine, and the official discrimination against the refugee himself, created pressures that served to perpetuate the notion in the mind of the young Palestinian that he was the member of a minority, thus enhancing his Palestinian consciousness. In his home a Palestinian child, whether born in Beirut, Amman, or Damascus, would be instructed to identify himself as a Palestinian from Haifa or Lydda or any other town that had been his parents' birthplace, and his own experience would constantly remind him of this.

If alienation breeds an attraction to radical ideology, then Palestinian youngsters found ample cause for incitement in their exclusion from society. They became the most left wing and revolutionary group in the Arab world, espousing progressive causes or extreme views that alarmed their parents and antagonized other Arabs. They rejected above all old political heroes, religious and class hierarchies, and the remote social, economic, and ideological values of yore.

But we are still in the 1950's, and the Palestinians, caught in a vicious bind, turned to the Arab leaders, and particularly to Nasser, to right the wrong committed against them.

Here we witness the most ruthless and mercenary display of the manipulation of one man's misfortune for the benefit of another. Politically, "usurped Palestine" became a catch phrase to use in speeches by government leaders with a thirst for prestige and popularity. Pronunciamentos about liberating Palestine were heard continually. "The noble cause" was given all the vehemence that radio commentators could muster and the fierce passion with which draconian threats were made against Israel, promising its ultimate destruction, was indeed frightening. All made, presumably, on behalf of the Palestinians. But except for the Arab masses, who loved these mendacities and diversions, and the Palestinians, who continued to wait, it was known to all that the Arab governments had put the solution of the Palestine issue at the bottom of their list of priorities.

As if life in a refugee camp was not sufficiently hard for the Palestinians, they were discriminated against on every level in Arab society. Before a refugee found and was accepted for employment, he was called upon to apply for a work permit. In Lebanon, for example, where discrimination was most blatant, this was virtually impossible to come by. To cross borders between Lebanon, Jordan, and Syria, and sometimes even from one town to another in the same country, to visit a relative or conduct business, a Palestinian was required to wait for a laissez-passer from the authorities. The issuance of this document was left to the discretion of local bureaucrats who obliged only when they saw fit—in a few weeks, a few months, or never. Socially, Palestinians were despised, persecuted, or at best ignored.

Again I want to indulge a recollection. This of the time I was a teenager in Beirut when one day I arrived home at the camp (our home was a damp mudhouse of two rooms where I also picked up asthma) to discover that a group of drunken policemen had forced their way in and beaten up my mother and two sisters, apparently for failing to produce an identity card or UNRWA card or some other wretched document. That incident may be taken as marking the day I started to hate with a passion that was lunatic in its intensity. I hated first the Arabs; then, in an inarticulate and vague manner, the world. A few days later I was near the Corniche, where I used to go to peddle chewing gum, and joined a crowd of onlookers watching a street entertainer with a performing monkey. The entertainer proceeded to tell his animal to "show us how a Palestinian picks up his food rations." I was a rough boy of fourteen, hardened to street life, but I could not suppress an outburst of tears. For that was a microcosm of the world, and I was too weak, too alone, to hit back at it, so I wept. We all, in a way, wept.

But the life of the Palestinians, as the 1960's opened, was no longer to be identified with stagnation, hate, and ignorance—contrary to the popular view of it held in the West. A great many refugees, although still adamant about refusing permanent absorption in their host countries, left the mud of the camps and found comfortable housing outside.° The opening up of employment opportunities for Palestinians in the oil-rich countries of the Gulf, and the aid given to them by UNRWA, drastically changed the tempo, if not the structure, of their lives. Their standard of living improved, and money arriving home from relatives working in the desert, supplemented by modest scholarships and various grants, enabled Palestinian youngsters to resume their studies. Education, probably seen as the only tangible investment for the future, became to a Palestinian family the most crucial and the most momentous accomplishment ever. There was nothing else a young Palestinian could hope for, cling to, touch with his being. We studied like ones possessed. To drop out of school, not to contemplate going to college, not to surpass the achievements of our Lebanese, Syrian, or Jordanian tormentors, was to us a stigma and a badge of shame. The Palestinians now have by far the highest literacy rate in the Middle East and 64,000 university graduates— only 3,000 graduates less than Israel (with a higher population)— were trained during the same period, between 1948 and 1967.†

° Over the years, refugees abandoned their camps in great numbers; about one-third, however, continue to live there. See Peter Dodd and Halim Barakat, *River Without Bridges* (Beirut: Institute for Palestine Studies, 1969).

† According to the 1966–1967 UNRWA report (p. 35), at least 75 percent of refugee children of school age were attending formal elementary and preparatory

Long before the close of the second decade of their dispersion in the Arab world, Palestinians were holding the most sensitive positions in technology and commerce, occupying the faculties of major universities in the Arab capitals, and becoming active in the arts, science and banking.

Then came the Six Day War, and many of us became refugees for the second time. The space that encompassed our fractured being became intolerable. The humble pie that we had eaten was no longer edible. Our dependence on disreputable Arab governments and an unsympathetic world became meaningless. The artificial and jargonized rhetoric from Arab leaders and commentators sitting behind their microphones became, in retrospect, nonsensical and empty.

We debunked the old values and the old ways, the old truths and the old irreconcilables, the old concerns and the old displacements, and re-examined the options. We were solving our own problem, in our own way, in our own time.

---

schools. Out of 120 countries reporting data to UNESCO, for the 1963–1964 period, the Palestinians ranked thirteenth—on a level with France and Czechoslovakia.

2. The Camp and the City

A breeze began to blow as we moved slowly along the coast road, heading to the Lebanese border—my mother and father, my two sisters, my brother and I. Behind us lay the city of Haifa, long the scene of bombing, sniper fire, ambushes, raids, and bitter fighting between Palestinians and Zionists. Before us lay the city of Sidon and indefinite exile. Around us the waters of the Mediterranean sparkled in the sun. Above us eternity moved on unconcerned, as if God in his heavens watched the agonies of men, as they walked on crutches, and smiled. And our world had burst, like a bubble, a bubble that had engulfed us within its warmth. From then on I would know only crazy sorrow and watch the glazed eyes of my fellow Palestinians burdened by loss and devastated by pain.

April 1948. And so it was the cruelest month of the year; but there were crueler months, then years.

Abba Eban, in his book *My People*, dismisses the Palestinians within quotation marks, and Golda Meir once demanded: "The Palestinians? Who are they? They don't exist!" But that was us streaming into Lebanon, Syria, and Jordan, with tales of horror, persecution, and fear, walking around in a daze, confronting one another with a set of baffling facts, but willing to wait for a few weeks, even months, to return to our towns, homes, shops, offices, and businesses. Gradually, Palestinians, finding themselves unwelcome guests in host countries with depressed economies reluctant to absorb or aid them, capitulated and started to line up each month at the newly set up UNRWA food depots. A great many refugees discovered themselves, in the very early stages of homelessness, if not already living in camps, surely gravitating toward them. Hunger, as only those who have felt the ache of hunger know, is a much more potent emotion than pride. The latter is violently smothered when one's sensibilities and intellect are engulfed by nothing other than a daily search for food, warm clothing, and satisfying the needs of a newly arrived baby. Destitution, unwarranted and inexplicable, had then started to leave its shattering effects on the very fabric of our beings.

After a few months in Sidon, we moved again, a Palestinian family of six heading to a refugee camp in Beirut, impotent with hunger, frustration, and incomprehension. But there we encountered other families equally helpless, equally baffled, who like us never had enough to eat, never enough to offer books and education to their children, never enough to face an imminent winter. In later years, when we left the camp and found better housing and a better life outside and grew up into our early teens, we would complain about not having this or that and would be told by our mothers: "You are well off, boy! Think of those still living there in the camps. Just think of them and stop making demands." We would look out the window and see the rain falling and hear the thunder. And we would remember. We would understand. We would relent as we thought "of those still living there."

Man adapts. We adapted, the first few months, to life in a refugee camp. In the adaptation we were also reduced as men, as women, as children, as human beings. At times we dreamed. Reduced dreams. Distorted ambitions. One day, we hoped, our parents would succeed in buying two beds for me and my sister to save us the agonies of asthma, intensified from sleeping on blankets on the cold floor. One day, we hoped, there would be enough to buy a few pounds of pears or apples as we had done on those special occasions when we fought and sulked and complained because one of us was given a smaller piece of fruit than the others. One day soon, we hoped, it would be the end of the month when the UNRWA rations arrived and there was enough to eat for a week. One day soon, we argued, we would be back in our homeland.

Old men would sit in the shade of nearby side-street cafes and discuss "our problem" and recount stories of martyrs who were killed off by the Turks, the British, and later the Zionists. Abu Salim, a well-known poet from Haifa, would sit amongst them to recite or, aided by a few glasses of arak, compose verses on Palestine. First Abu Salim would walk down the path, in the early evening, followed by a horde of kids reverently whispering "Salam alleik, salam alleik," and sit at his favorite table and await his narjeel. Soon the men from the other cafes would go over to join him.

He would say little as he sucked at his pipe and took an occasional sip at his drink (he was a Christian), but at that break in the conversation or the heated passion when the men would fall silent to add a burning coal to their narjeels, he would read his lines to us till the late hours. The moths would gather around the kerosene lamps and the men would mumble between verses "Ya leil, ya aein" (my night, my mind—they have fused). It is a typical Palestinian night, Palestinian mind. And we would know we were together in a transplanted village that once was on the road to Jaffa, that once was in the north of Haifa, that once was close to Lydda.

For if we had indeed acquired that "hate and bitterness" that the Western world claimed we were reputed for, we also danced the dabke, played the oud, and the women worked their embroidery. And those people outside the camp (not to mention the Western "tourists" with their blessed sympathy, their cameras, their sociology degrees, and their methodological and statistical charts), seeing our tattered rags hanging on us like white flags of surrender, but not hearing our "ya leil, ya aein," did not know what we had. A feeling within us. Growing. A hope. A hope. The sad feeling of seeing a star, alone, at dawn. The waiting at a gap between the onrush of sounds. The observer, enriched, becoming the observed.

Next to us there lived a middle-aged woman, Um Ismael, who made a living selling her embroidery in the streets of downtown Beirut. Her volatile temper and strong language usually got her in trouble with the authorities. On top of the offense she committed in not having a license to peddle, she was wont to challenge the police, at times using her fists, and call them "useless sons of whores"—for she had acquired the notion (and in those days she was decidedly out of her mind) that the Lebanese were in collusion with the Zionists to crush and degrade the Palestinian people. Um Ismael would from time to time rush to the camp after work and explain how she had seen a convoy of army trucks and tanks heading south.

"Where else would the sons of whores be going, I ask you? Now I ask you?" she would demand, gesticulating wildly. "I tell you those sons of whores are going south to help the Zionists. We have to stop those bastards, I say. Don't you remember the British and the arms they were moving up to Mount Carmel every day?"

Once three army trucks were passing by the camp, possibly on their way to Sidon or further south to Tyre, and there was Um Ismael hurling rocks, garbage, and obscenities at them before she was forcibly restrained. Luckily the occupants, peasant soldiers from the Bika, were more frightened of the mad Palestinians crowding around than the gendarmes would have been, so no confrontation ensued. After these violent outbursts Um Ismael would always break down and sob, mumbling pathetically about how the

Zionists killed her husband, Abu Ismael, and left her alone in the world. Um Yacoub, with whom she lived, would drag her away; soon she would dry her tears and revert to her old defiant abusive self, especially if Um Yacoub, who espoused our own version of a *Reader's Digest* optimism and faith in life, would interject a comforting remark.

"Calm down, Um Ismael, remember the evil you do will be punished by God. He will help us if we are patient, if we are calm."

"Ben sharmoota on my evil! What about God's evil? Be calm you say; didn't you see those dirty sons of whores going south with ammunition and arms to the Zionists?"

"I saw them; maybe . . ."

"I saw the sons; I saw them, I tell you."

"Be calm now, Um Ismael, please . . ."

"Ben sharmoota on my calm. I tell you those sons of whores are against us. The whole world is against us."

The days stretched into months and those into a year and yet another. Kids would play in the mud of the winters and the dust of the summers, while "our problem" was debated at the UN and moths died around the kerosene lamps. A job had been found for me in a factory not far from the camp, where I worked for six months. I felt pride in the fact that I was a bread earner and was thus eligible to throw my weight around the house, legitimately demand an extra spoonful of sugar in my tea, and have my own money to spend on comic books and an occasional orange on the side. I had even started saving to buy my own bed, but I was fired soon after that.

A kid at work had called me a two-bit Palestinian and a fist fight ensued. The supervisor, an obese man with three chins and a green stubble that covered most of his face and reached under his eyes, came over to stop the fight. He decided I had started it all, slapped me hard twice, deducted three lira from my wages for causing trouble (I earned seven lira a week), paid me the rest, called me a two-bit Palestinian, and, pointing to my blond hair, suggested I had a whore mother and shoved me out the door.

I went to the river and sat on the grass to eat my lunch. I was shaken more by the two-bit-Palestinian epithet than by the plight of being unemployed. At home and around the camp, we had unconsciously learned to be proud of where we came from and to continue remembering that we were Palestinians. If this was stigmatic outside, there it was an identity to be known, perpetuated, embraced. My father, reproaching us for an ignoble offense of some kind, would say: "You are a Palestinian." He would mean: as a Palestinian one is not expected to stoop that low and betray his tradition. If we came home affecting a Lebanese accent, our mother would say: "Hey, what's wrong with your own accent? You're too good for your own people or something? You want to sound like a foreigner when we return to Haifa? What's wrong with you, hey?"

I was seething with indignation and was determined to return to the factory and get into another fist fight, this time with the supervisor himself. I walked back and stood outside the office, which was on the ground floor and had a large window overlooking the street. I picked up a rock and started calling for the man to come out.

"Where are you, greasy two-bit Lebanese, come out, you son; come out, son."

My excitement brought on a sudden attack of asthma and I was beginning to wonder whether this was an opportune moment for a fight. "Come out you son of a whore," I persisted. The supervisor put his head out and began to say something, but when he saw me rushing in his direction with every intention of throwing the rock at him, he retreated inside the sanctuary of his office. The rock went through the open window. Maybe it hit the plaster reproduction of St. Alexis that he had hanging on the wall, or the cherished framed pictures of members of his family. Although he knew where I lived, I am sure he knew better than to come chasing after me at the camp. He would have been torn to pieces by my elder brother, his friends, or whoever happened to be there and realized that he was a Lebanese and what he wanted; and a Palestinian accent was not easy to affect. In those days the only strangers who ventured into the camps were cops, invariably

drunken ones at that and in groups. That night at the cafe I gave
an account of my venture at the match factory and Abu Salim
asked my father, as he scratched under his checkered headdress,
"How old is your boy, Abu Khaled?" ° When told I was ten years
old, he said cryptically, "That's good, good."

For the next five months I floated around the camp and walked
the streets in the city; I also started stealing from shops and getting into brawls, mostly with a group of boys from Baalbek who
lived a kilometer or two down from the camp. Um Yacoub's son,
Youssef, and I attached ourselves to a gang called Awlad Falasteen. We used to meet up at the Karamat hill to watch the foot-
ball games and snatch lunch baskets from the stands. We became
so daring and blatant at doing the latter that sometimes we would
walk up to a group sitting on the grass, quietly relieve them of
their food packs, and run away. Occasionally a cop would manage
to catch one or two of us and we would get viciously beaten on
the spot and let go. In the fifties the Lebanese did not practice the
niceties of laws governing arrest, offense, trials, and detention.

In the summer Youssef and I got into what we considered a
good thing, operating at the St. Simone beach, which was patronized exclusively by Americans, British, and other Europeans (diplomatic staff, businessmen, personnel from the oil companies in
the Gulf) and was usually fenced in and off limits to nonmembers,
i.e., natives. We used to go there, sit on the other side of the fence,
and wait around until the beach got crowded. I would undress
down to my trunks, go into the water, and swim over to the other
side and walk around. Because of my blond hair I was easily taken
for a European and was thus never called upon to explain my
presence to the Lebanese attendants and lifeguards. Within a few
minutes my trained eye would spot those couples leaving their
beach umbrellas to go in for their splash, giggling and laughing,
their bodies glistening with suntan oil, their faces healthy with

---

° "Abu" in Arabic means "father of." In Palestinian society a man is addressed
as Abu followed by the name of his eldest son. Similarly with the title "Um" which
means "mother of." Surnames prefixed by Mr. or Mrs. are rarely used except for
purposes of documental identification.

patches of red from good beer or a good diet, and I would go there with the confidence that only a child of ten could have, wrap everything in the towel conveniently left behind, and calmly head toward the fence to throw the stuff over to Youssef.

"Bravo alleik, bravo!" he would say.

"I can do two more jobs, I think; wait on."

"Bravo alleik, bravo alleik."

We would return to the camp on the bus and sit in an abandoned hut near the water pump and examine our booty. There would be money, watches, cigarettes, books, cameras, fountain pens, lighters, and an excessive number of towels. The latter we could not sell and we gave them away. I gave one large one in particular to the owner of the cafe at the camp. It had words printed on it in English that he translated as saying it was the property of the U.K. government.

"It could be the words mean the U.K. embassy," he said. "I am not sure. The sons. I like it." He used it to wear around his middle as an apron, and in later months when it got tattered, used it to wipe the tables.

Youssef and I, along with some of the boys from Awlad Falasteen, also used to go to Ras Beirut, the rich area north of the city where affluent Lebanese families never tired, and still do not, of emulating Western habits and adopting Western fashions. If we did not go into busy shops to steal chocolate, tinned food, and other goods, we would walk down the zig-zag, off the lighthouse, to the beach and hang around there to talk and swim. Lying on the sand we would argue over how far the Palestinian border was from Beirut, the things we did and the schools we went to back home, and the girls at the camp.

It did not take long for my parents to discover the truth behind some of the nefarious activities I indulged in with Youssef and Awlad Falasteen and I was soon limited to an area in close proximity to the camp. I pondered the possibility of employment and decided to become a bread earner again through more conventional means than the precarious career of stealing. One day, with all the money I had then, I bought a carton of 500 packages of chewing gum and became a peddler around the Corniche, the

Borj and later, when I was more settled, outside the gates of the American University of Beirut.

Every morning I would take the tram to Ras Beirut, jumping off at every stop to elude the conductor, and push my goods to students. I discovered the virtues of the hard sell, which involved chasing after a customer, not taking no for an answer, and bugging him into parting with five piasters for a packet.° Occasionally an irate student would give me a shove or two, but that was the sort of business I was in.

I was beginning to make a lot of money, nearly three times as much as at the match factory. I would go home before it got dark, taking the tram, again dodging conductors—an art I became more daringly adept at as time went on. I would get off as the tram reached a stop, case the two carriages, examining the spot where the conductor of each was engaged, and select the most strategic of the four doors to jump back on again. At home I would sit on my bed and feel the joy of taking piles of coins out of my pocket and counting them.

But my ventures into the realms of business as a successful entrepreneur of chewing gum were cut short. A small ad had appeared in the paper which caught my father's attention, inviting children of Palestinian refugees to attend a free school run by an evangelist organization. The only price to pay, it transpired, was to kneel in prayer for an aggregate of forty-five minutes each day and open your heart so the love of Jesus could get in and learn that we sinners were saved only because He sacrificed his life for us.

My parents were incoherent with excitement, for my sister and I could go to school at last (my elder brother was now working for an oil company in Saudi Arabia).† I was equally exhilarated by

---

° One hundred piasters equal one lira. A lira is worth about $.32.

† In the middle fifties, with the increase in oil production in the Arabian Peninsula, Kuwait, and the Gulf Protectorates, there was a great demand for labor. The oil companies had no difficulty recruiting candidates among the Palestinians, who were the most educated community in the Arab world. Hence Aramco and the other big concerns had a higher percentage of Palestinians on their staffs than others. However, political considerations were also decidedly involved, for it was be-

being able to do something so exotic and so exclusive as going to school. My memory of St. Lux Primary in Haifa had become remote and alien, like the dreams I desperately tried to recapture upon waking, when I had been the proud owner of brand new comic books and bags of fruit and cookies.

I was the first one up around the house the next day to remind my sister of where we were going. When we arrived at the address given in the ad, we were met by a middle-aged lady from Haifa, with whom my father initially spent twenty minutes talking about "our problem," the UN debate that had taken place recently over the refugees, and reminiscing on old days, places and events, feeling sure the future held good things in store for us and it definitely would not be long before we all returned to our homeland. There was a bond and a warmth between the two strangers—they were fellow Palestinians and fellow *déracinés*. Whenever Palestinians met in those days they would reach out to touch that vibration of intimacy, the sharing of a pain now blinding the eyes, and the intangible qualities of mind that made "us" and excluded "them." We became close, reached closer, as if to be equals in the sharing of our burden, our loss. The formalities that had distinguished or separated us in Palestine—the intellectual from the semi-literate, the professional from the artisan, the middle class from the upper class, the rich from the poor, the pious from the unbeliever, the Christian from the Moslem—were imperceptibly dropped.

Once when I was peddling chewing gum, I had run after a student asking him to buy. He turned around and, recognizing my accent, asked me if I was a Palestinian. When I said yes, he patted me very gently and very lovingly on the shoulder.

"Yirda alleik, ben," he said, giving me some money.

"God bless you too, brother," I said after him. And I felt it

---

lieved that if Palestinian youth continued to find no employment opportunities in economically hard-pressed Syria and Jordan and paranoically sectarian Lebanon, this would ultimately become a potential danger to Arab societies. In the year 1958 Aramco, for example, had 76 percent of its Arab staff (excluding Saudis) composed of Palestinians. By 1968, with the change in the political developments and the emergence of a hyperactive and revolutionary fedayeen movement, Palestinians were being "surplused" in great numbers and few were being hired.

then; for it was within me—our individual suffering extended and identified as a group suffering that also embraced those others whose sensibilities were smothered and whose souls were degraded. I recall, years later, when I was at the beach with a group of Lebanese I knew from Ras Beirut and spotted a Jewish friend of mine sitting on the sand by himself and asked him to come and join us. When the fellow's identity was revealed his fellow Lebanese became hostile, addressing him as if the responsibilities of Zionism were his, as if he were uncomplainingly to carry the burden of exclusion, and carry it under the chin. In a moment of incomprehension (for so it seemed to me in those days) I became a Jew, the Jew became a Palestinian, bound into a commonwealth of peoples heavily laden, heavily oppressed. My hate for the bourgeois Arab and his value structure, whether I viewed them in a political context or not, intensified further. The irony of my plight was that as I grew up my bogeyman was not the Jew (despite the incessant propaganda that Radio Cairo subjected us to), nor was he the Zionist (if indeed I recognized the distinction), nor was he for that matter the imperialist or the Western supporters and protectors of the state of Israel, but he was the Arab. The Arab in the street who asked if you'd ever heard the one about the Palestinian who . . . The Arab at the Aliens Section who wanted you to wait obsequiously for your work permit, the Arab at the police station who felt he possessed a carte blanche to mistreat you, the Arab who rejected you and, most crucially, took away from you your sense of hope and sense of direction. He was the bogeyman you saw every morning and every night and every new year of every decade tormenting you, reducing you, dehumanizing you, and confirming your servitude. To the Palestinian, the young Palestinian, living and growing up in Arab society, the Israeli was the enemy in the mathematical matrix; we never saw him, lived under his yoke, or, for many of us, remembered him. Living in a refugee camp and going hungry, we felt that the causes of our problem were abstract, the causes of its perpetuation were real.

Our Palestinian consciousness, instead of dissipating, was enhanced and acquired a subtle nuance and a new dimension. It was buoyed by two concepts: the preservation of our memory of Palestine and our acquisition of education. We persisted in refusing the houses and monetary compensation offered by the UN to settle us in our host countries. We wanted nothing short of returning to our homeland. And from Syria, Lebanon, and Jordan, we would see, a few miles, a few yards, across the border, a land where we had been born, where we had lived, and where we felt the earth. "This is my land," we would shout, or cry, or sing, or plead, or reason. And to that land a people had come, a foreign community of colonizers, aided by a Western world in a hurry to rid itself of guilt and shame, demanding independence from history, from heaven, and from us.

I went to school every day with my sister, opening my heart for forty-five minutes to let the love of Jesus seep in and learn about the sacrifice that He made so that we sinners could live—and then to classes. I loved school like few kids ever loved school. The excitement of reading aloud, gloating over homework, rehearsing for a play, being first in class, reading books that were all one's own to touch and smell and reread; and to feel the power, arrogantly displayed at home, of adding and multiplying, of conjugating irregular verbs, of reciting a poem, of knowing the whereabouts of Indonesia, of recounting the exploits of Napoleon.

When summer came I looked around for work, but the indignity of packing matchboxes, peddling chewing gum, or stealing was not for a man of my endowments any more. I knew where the money was, and I was aiming high. Once when I was walking along the Corniche I had noticed a select swimming club that was patronized almost exclusively by Americans and British, outside which I figured I would launch an enterprise of sorts. So with all my savings in my pocket one sunny morning, I proceeded to the club searching for the nearest bakery on the way. There I bought twenty kaakis (hollowed-out pieces of rye bread with a hint of spices and egg in them), rented a tray and an adjustable stand for it, and set up shop at the entrance to the swimming club.

Within a few minutes a middle-aged Lebanese, who I discovered later was the attendant in the locker room, walked by, looked back hesitantly, and then started screaming with all his might. The fury in his voice was indeed frightening.

"You mob of useless sons of whores. I told you before, didn't I, I told you you were not allowed around here. Come on, get moving before I break your neck." The man's face had turned red, and as he seemed on the verge of striking me, I was too petrified to move. I was also loath to open my mouth as he surely would have recognized my accent and then felt compelled, or at least free, to knock me about. "Come on, move, get on with it you son of a whore before I throw you and all this shit into the water."

"Yes, sir," I said.

"Well come on. Why do you keep coming here? I told you, you mob of dirty swine, to clear out of here."

As he continued to give free vent to his anger, while I fumbled with my tray and its stand, which at that dangerous moment got stuck, I saw Mr. Des McMeekin walking up the stairs. Mr. McMeekin, a kindly soul from Kansas who used to come to our school to act as a speaker at the let's-kneel-in-prayer morning sessions and who used to pat the students on the head and whisper "Jesus loves you" in their ears, recognized me and interceded on my behalf, telling the man his anger was completely unwarranted.

"I know this boy," he said when he realized what the trouble was. "He is a student at one of our schools. I vouch for his integrity and I shall contact Mr. Abbas in connection with granting this child permission to continue his innocuous activities here. In the meantime, I will suggest that you refrain from intimidating him any further."

I worked there for well over two months. I did not do well the first few days, but as I became well known as a permanent fixture at the entrance, exchanging pleasantries with swimmers, some of whom called me by name, business picked up. At weekends I used to have to return to the bakery several times to replenish supplies. The locker attendant, whose name was Anton, became reluctantly friendly and left me alone. My connection with Mr. McMeekin, and my popularity with many of the members, were awe-inspiring for him. But I did not like his habit of coming up to my tray, helping himself to a kaaki or two every day, and not paying for them.

He obviously felt entitled to a kickback. Once he and his two sons, whom he brought with him to the club, stopped by and each helped themselves to one of my kaakis.

One of his two boys, who was about my age, associating the status of a Palestinian, particularly a Palestinian peddler, with the lowliest of the low, treated me condescendingly and as one of his servants that day, and asked me to go and buy him a bottle of fizzy drink. I told him I was busy.

"Ya?" he inquired. "Well, I want you to go buy me a bottle of fizz now."

"I am working, can't you see?"

"Well, if you don't I'll tell my dad."

"Get the hell away from me, son of a whore."

He ran down the stairs but didn't emerge again until they were ready to leave.

Anton at least did not make a fuss when I went to swim during the innumerable breaks from work. I would splash my way to the raft, a hundred yards off the diving board, and lie back with my feet in the water thinking of the adventure stories I had been reading by H. Rider Haggard and Ben Battoota and having fantasies of the day when we would return to Haifa where no one would say two-bit Palestinian because everyone would be a Palestinian.

Things were getting very awkward for money around the house, for although my brother was now working in Dhahran, Saudi Arabia, and sending most of his pay home, expenses had multiplied. With the improvement in our standard of living (we had moved out of the camp) there was an increase in the cost of it. We were forever making demands which of course were never met. This would be justified by the fact that we were refugees and that we were to be patient until we returned to our homeland.

We were refugees. That was all. They were supposed to be magic words to explain the unexplainable. We were learning, feeling, what the words meant. We were aliens. Pariahs. Untouchables. We were apart. But deep in our psyches, deep in our consciousness, we wanted to remain apart and hold on dearly, aggressively, to what we had left. We were not surrendering those intangibles that made us relate to all our fellow Palestinians wherever they may have been, and bespoke the dimension of our problem. We held on, standing against a wall, imprisoned within the confines of our frustrations.

We held on. The Turks for hundreds of years had ruled over us, desperate to impose their traditions of cruelty and terror and rob us of our linguistic and cultural heritage. But our language and our culture came through unscathed. There were those in the Arab world who used us, spoke on our behalf, and had a great time coining a whole heap of phrases that told of the doom awaiting the usurpers of our land. Fierce passions were demonstrated here, violent threats were made there, and inevitable unity was to come about everywhere. And forever the promise that Palestine will soon be liberated and the Zionist colonizers driven out (into the sea, no less). No leader made a speech that he considered appealing to the masses without reference to "usurped Palestine" and the rights of its refugees.

This was carried to lunatic extremes, with the Arabic language lending itself well to those who could use impassioned rhetoric and manipulate its sonorous words. Many are the men who sob uncontrollably at poetry readings, at commemorations, or as they listen to speakers who have mastered their classical tongue and can sing its wealth of words. It is not essentially the words in our language that are in themselves effective, it is not what they signify or even the ideas they create. It is the sound of them that overwhelms the senses, engulfing the space within the listener and around him, invoking glories of olden times and touchable concepts of the freedom in the desert and supermen fighters who swarmed across the Levant to conquer the Byzantine and Persian empires. Words in a language that has remained virtually intact as pre-Islamic Arabs had used it.

Some of the best lines in Arabic poetry are untranslatable into other languages. They become gibberish or at best meaningless. Here is one that an Arab would recite aloud, stretching a word, shortening another, leaving a gap, then yet another word. And the words register not a symbol, not a transmuted message or an understanding of an abstraction, but an echo in the consciousness that only an Arab feels vibrating in his being.

> I know; I know the herd and the night and the wadi,
> I know; I know the sword and the lance and the paper
> and the plume.°

I left the Evangelists and with a scholarship from our contemptuous stepmother, UNRWA, enrolled in a high school run by a Palestinian organization. I stayed there until graduation. The schools that UNRWA sponsored were designed—unwittingly or not, no one can say—to raise Palestinian children on, and educate them in, accepting their plight in life as a preordained thing. They degraded the minds of Palestinian youngsters and trained, indeed pressured, them into viewing their reality as the norm of existence, never transcendable in its dimensions. They were taught about and given as a model a world where their destiny was left in the hands of others; a world and a society with directions that they did not understand and were growing up unable to reconcile to the order they saw around them. No attempt was made to explain the situation and the forces behind it that ruled their lives, or how they were to respond to them. They were thus made more defenseless. No courses were offered to show where they came from, the history of Palestine, who the Jews, who the Zionists, who the Arabs were. No reasons were offered to explain why Palestinian children were studying the American Civil War, the invasion of Russia by Napoleon, and the defeat of the Spanish Armada—rather than the story of their own civilization and cultural heritage, so rich in literature and ideas.

° This is my translation of two lines from a poem by Abu Al-Ala Al-Maarri, a famous Arab poet who died in 965 A.D. The authorized translation was made by E. G. Brown and is rendered thus (in *Literary History of Persia* [London: Cambridge University Press, 1929], Vol. I, p. 369): "I am known to the horse troop, the night, and the desert's expanse;/Not more to paper and pen than to sword and the lance." The two lines hinge on the verb "to know" (*yaref*), which in Arabic means more than "to be acquainted with" and carries the sense of knowledge as well as having feeling and a wonder for. The perception the poet invoked in the word *yaref* is not rendered in E. G. Brown's version. Nor is it in mine.

Before long I became active in politics (it was common practice for high school students to be as involved as their counterparts at universities) and acquired views hostile to Nasserism. I was disenchanted with the way the "Palestine problem" was being manipulated by leaders with mercenary ends in mind, and could see through some of the mendacities that were then shamelessly mouthed by responsible heads of government. I was reading voraciously: history, politics, economics, and fiction. I was getting bored with school work, which I considered simple or simplistic, and with knowing as a foregone conclusion that I would get high marks for term exams in most subjects.

I joined the Parti Syrien Nationaliste, which advocated socialism and union of the Levantine countries—whose people the party maintained had always shared their culture, destiny, and struggle for independence—and excluded the Egyptians and other North Africans from their scheme of things.

It was obvious to me in those days that the Egyptians, who had never considered themselves Arabs before, had come on the scene to satisfy their statesmen's political ambitions for leadership of the Arab world and of pan-Arabism. I was repelled most of all by their distasteful propaganda campaigns, with all the lies about their efforts to bring about a just solution of the Palestinian refugee problem. Their concern lay elsewhere, in other fields; the Palestinian issue, which had become "sacred," "noble," "a struggle to the death," was only an academic issue espoused for exploitative reasons. Mine had become not just a dispassionate renunciation of Nasserism, but almost a hate bordering on the personal.

All around me I could see Nasserites with a blind faith in the efficacy of words, words that had now become a torrent washing over the Middle East from Cairo. They were driving the British out of Egypt, they were facing up to the might of the imperialist world, they were effecting a union with Syria (and soon with the rest of the Arab world), they were well known and respected on the circuit of the nonaligned nations, they were loved by Tito and Sukarno, they were going to drive the Jews into the sea, they were running the Canal and had wrought economic wonders in their country.

And the Palestinians, awed, enchanted, and wallowing in the splendor of good days that were soon to be here again, lived for the day when Nasser would liberate their homeland.

At home there were tense scenes when I would argue mercilessly with my poor father, ridiculing his naive grasp of Middle Eastern politics, or, in desperation, rip Nasser's picture off the wall and spit on it. In my bitterness and innocence I did not give the unhappy man the chance to hold on to that symbol of hope he saw in the picture of the smiling face on the wall. In those days of emotional crisis, in those last years of his on earth, he had nothing except hope. And he hoped. And a million people hoped. And I relentlessly attacked him, robbing him of that system of logic he had constructed around himself to interpret the tragedy that had befallen him and his people.

I grow sick with anguish. I grow sick with heavens. I grow. And I see my father, muttering "Yirda alleik, ben," his hair the color of snow, sitting in the corner of a room reading a letter from my brother, with the rain falling on the roof.

He looks up. "Have you given your sister her lesson?"

Yes dad. Yes. Yes. I have given her a lesson. I have given a million lessons to a million sisters. A million sisters I have, walking barefoot on the cold floors of mudhouses in DP camps waiting for the end of the month to eat their rations of onions and beans and dip their bread in milk. I have a million sisters, dad, with a million simple dreams and a million simple memories. They are frightened not of the dark, these sisters, but of the cold. They knew not the sharing of humanity, but the nuances of despair. A million sisters, Yirda alleik, dad, who are unhappy.

I am old in my teens. And the Western world sees me and us all as wild-eyed illiterate Bedouins roaming the desert, or packed in ghettos, too backward to rise above our squalor, to transcend our lot. The Israelis present the image of the suntanned sabras making the desert flower, and the romance of the kibbutz in a land where Leon Uris was indeed on the ball.

I was becoming emotionally involved in active politics and joined innumerable demonstrations, some of which turned sour and provoked brutal police intervention. I had not been arrested yet, although I was hit on the head and shoulders a few times. But there were demonstrations and demonstrations, and some were fun. The visit John Foster Dulles paid to Beirut in the late fifties brought out a large crowd who marched from the American University gate, singing and shouting anti-American slogans, to the Foreign Ministry, where an official addressed us briefly, commending Lebanon for having laws protecting our freedom of expression and imploring us to go home. Everybody did. I had brought my swimming trunks with me and returned to the University on the tram (still dodging conductors) and walked down the campus paths to the student swimming club. I made a point of saying hello and speaking to people I knew there, to let them hear how hoarse my voice was. It was my badge of courage. They knew where I had been.

Another event that attracted a large crowd was the gathering at a cemetery for the burial ceremonies of a student who had died from bullet wounds at a demonstration (which I had not attended because of its pro-Nasser orientation). This was not fun. The police assigned to guard against disorder were standing there facing a crowd which associated them with the slaying of their fellow student. Before long someone threw the first stone and hell broke loose in a phantasmagoric scene of police chasing students running among gravestones and taking cover behind epitaphs.

I was never into demonstrations aimed at the ubiquitous United States Information Service or at breaking Embassy glass. I used the facilities of the former and could never bring myself to do the latter.

In one demonstration, one that was also fun and in which I picked up a surfeit of hoarseness, I led the boys from our high school, walking erect and carrying a flag (I forget which), to meet up with the detachment from another school outside their gate. When we arrived I got into an argument with the headmaster, intimidating him with the flag pole. He looked at me angrily, and with the best choice of words in classical Arabic, said: "Alas for a nation, indeed alas, that owns sons of your kind."

"I belong to no nation, sir."

"You are an Arab, are you not?" he demanded indignantly.

"No, sir, I am a Palestinian."

"Alas, then, for that nation."

Alas indeed. Amen.

One of the last demonstrations I joined before leaving high school had dramatic repercussions. It was a very large demonstration, and, as it was in support of the Algerian Revolution, it attracted people with different shades of ideology. There were Arab Nationalists, Nasserites, Parti Syrien people, Communists, and others who were not normally involved but felt called upon to join. The only group which refused to take part were the rightwing reactionaries of the Falangist movement, led by Pierre Jemayel, who emulated the French in mannerisms and behavior and whose rallying cry was: "Lebanon (*Grand Liban*) for the Lebanese." It was said on campus in those days that a Falangist would kiss your behind if you paid him the compliment of saying you thought him a Frenchman. Unlike most of us mortals, not finding it difficult enough being members of one world, they also wanted to be members of another—the world of our colonial oppressors, to be sure.

We congregated calmly, again outside the gate of the American University, and marched through downtown Beirut to a spot near the Foreign Ministry where student leaders made speeches extolling the noble war the guerrillas were waging against the French and the solidarity of the Arab peoples who were behind the Algerians all the way. It was a peaceful gathering and, because of the clear cut, uncontroversial nature of the cause, little heated passion was aroused. The press, the middle classes, and the government were in sympathy with the demonstration and in support of the guerrillas. When the speeches were over, and the boys were going home or heading to the beaches, a Nationalist, a Palestinian senior at the University who was well known for his activism (Palestinians formed a majority of the agitators on the campus), invited all those interested to come to the movement's city headquarters for more speeches.

I went along with a couple of my friends, taking a short cut through the back streets. The Arab Nationalists lecture hall and information center were part of the second floor, above a movie house, of an office building with gaudy signs all over its front advertising the names of its occupants. There were doctors' clinics, tailors, lawyers, travel agents, a night school, a coffee house, a bank, and an organization called the Joint Christian Committee.

About two hundred people arrived, almost all of whom were students, and filled the hall in less than half an hour. The senior, whose name was Khaled ben Youssef, went straight to the point and exhorted us to reflect upon the virtues of our struggle against imperialism, the suffering that the Arabs had to endure under the Turks, the British, and the French, and our land usurped by the Zionists. He praised Nasser and the battle for independence in the Maghreb, condemned the reactionary and feudal regimes that remained in the Arab world, and called for an enhanced level of awareness among students of issues that confronted our region.

He was an articulate and eloquent speaker who was very much at home in his classical Arabic. "The land of the Arabs is for the Arabs," he thundered, to receive a long minute or two of applause. And when that subsided, he would begin again: "The land of the Arabs is for the Arabs," only to be interrupted again with more applause.

Other but less effective speakers followed, virtually reiterating what ben Youssef had said, and the audience was getting a little bored. Some of those who were sitting nearest to the door sneaked out. It was getting dark outside and the reflection of colored neon lights was flickering on and off the glass of the hall windows. I was leaning over to ask someone for a cigarette when word came that the police were surrounding the room and the building. They claimed ours was an unlawful assembly, as no permission had been granted for our political meeting, and demanded that we surrender our names, addresses, and fingerprints, among other things, after which we were to be allowed to go home.

Ben Youssef immediately took over and maintained that the hall was private property, that we were committing no offense, and that we were not voluntarily giving in. "Never," he shouted, and the crowd applauded. The events in the hall had been a bit of a bore up until then, and now a hint of danger was introduced which suddenly infused the evening with the thrill of the unexpected.

Word was passed back of our decision to defy the police and stay put. Everybody relaxed, put their feet up on chairs, lay on the floor, or went out on the balcony to shout slogans or piss over the railing. In the middle of the night, Mr. Kassab, a respected and popular professor, turned up to speak to us. He explained that he was with us but that we ought to do what was expected by the authorities and that he had been assured by the police that no action was going to be taken against us, no prosecution and no intimidation. They merely wanted our particulars and fingerprints for their records.

"Never," ben Youssef shouted.

"Never," we shouted back.

"Good luck," shouted Mr. Kassab, and left dejectedly.

At dawn the police seemed to have had enough. They passed the word that unless we did what they demanded, they were coming into the hall to put us all under arrest. We still refused.

When they came in we were ready for them. We offered no resistance. We were tired and sleepy and wanted to go home, after having had all the fun we required. The men who barged into the hall to pick us up were soldiers, short young peasants from the mountains with bewildered faces and apprehensive eyes. They looked more uncertain than we did. The soldier who ushered me from the room, down the stairs to a waiting army van, twisting my right arm behind my back and walking me in front of him, looked decidedly frightened. I tried to engage him in conversation on the way, but he was too nervous to speak.

We were taken to a military jail near the Rawshi beach, outside Beirut, where they herded us into large cells and locked us in. In a few hours, when everybody had been safely put behind bars, they proceeded to take us upstairs in batches of ten to take our fingerprints and pictures for their records. One kid, still with great reserves of energy despite fatigue and lack of sleep, wanted to be facetious and made a face at the camera before his picture was taken. A cop walked over and grabbed him violently by the scruff of the neck and said: "Sit up straight, son of a whore, or I'll bash your head in." The kid did just that. There were no more similar antics.

As no one could say what was to become of us, or how long we were to be behind bars, and as few of us had had much sleep, a mood of despondency reigned. There was little talk. Cigarettes, books, and periodicals were at a premium.

In the evening we were taken, again in groups of ten, to line up outside a room on the second floor of the jail where we were to be interrogated and sign statements. We all had agreed to say that we were passing by the building where the meeting was held, heard noise, walked up to investigate, and sat down to listen to the talk. We were not politically active and had no connection with the nationalists.

The interrogators mechanically asked us a few stock questions and made us sign forms before they waved us through wearily. We still did not know when we were getting out. A few rich kids whose fathers had hired attorneys and who had been taken to a special room to be interviewed, told us they were assured we would be out the following day. We slept on the floor, using blankets the guards supplied. Most of us were up at dawn to grumble about the weather, the condition of the cell, the facilities, and life in general. Some viciously blamed the Nationalists for getting us into a mess, others blamed the police for making a fuss of an innocuous gathering of students who wanted to listen to political speeches.

The Palestinians were getting uneasy as word was passed that only Lebanese nationals would be released. And sure enough, at about eleven o'clock all the Lebanese students were let out. The rest waited for two more hours before something happened. There were five or six Syrians and a handful of Jordanians; the rest were Palestinians. These latter were made to sign an additional statement disavowing any further attempts at involvement in politics or else be subject to deportation. The police official responsible for Palestinian affairs lectured us on the evils of meddling in the internal life of the state of Lebanon, and reminded us that we were aliens living in the country under duress. Pointing a hairy finger with a big ugly ring on it, he threatened that should our names occur on their records again, indicating any further political agitation, we would surely be deported.

One kid of sixteen raised his hand, as if he were in a classroom, and asked earnestly: "Where will we be deported to, sir?"

"Never mind where you will be deported to, son of a whore, just do as you're told."

Before the day was out everybody had gone home. Ben Youssef's men returned to campus a few days later and said he had been beaten up by the police and was likely to be in jail for a long time, and later prosecuted on a variety of charges.

The political cell I ran for the Parti Syrien was expanding rapidly and we had to split it into two. The leadership of the new cell was given to Samir, a Palestinian kid whose family lived at a refugee camp in Baalbek and who was in Beirut on a special grant. He had far outstripped the students, and, it was rumored, the teachers, at his UNRWA school and special arrangements had been made to have him sent to a better school in the city. There was no doubt that he had an intelligence quotient nearing the genius mark.

Before we broke up to form the two cells, we used to meet in his room, near the lighthouse, every Thursday after classes. Our activities in the cell were quite innocuous. One of us, who would have been assigned the job the week before, would read out details of the political events of the week in the Arab world and we would discuss their significance and try to glean the truth behind them. Each member would be called upon to give an account of his proselytizing at the school and elsewhere. Teachers with known reactionary views would be mentioned and strategy for attacking them mapped. If a demonstration or protest was imminent, a review of its function and value would ensue. Word as to whether we would join it or not would ultimately come from above, but no resentment or chastisement would be directed against a member who felt, in all sincerity, that he could not take part or that the cause was not being furthered by it. Rarely, though, was there any violent disagreement among us.

From time to time the coordinator (a much older student, usually an undergraduate at the American University), who was responsible for five or six cells, would come by to attend a meeting. He was not identified as to his position and was supposed to be known only to the head of the cell, but in actual fact everyone knew who he was, for in his presence those who had been lax in manifesting their pride in the Arabic language and culture by using English words here and there (because they had no Arabic equivalent) would go through agonies to avoid them. Arabic language and culture, in our cell, in our party, in our life, became a fetish. It was considered contemptible to discard our own linguistic and national heritage to embrace another, especially if it belonged to our former oppressors, French or British. We were to excel, by all means, in mastering the oppressor's language and in learning his ways and his literature and his know-how, but we were not to emulate him, for that was demeaning. We would boycott cafes around school or the University with names like "Uncle Sam's" and "Queen's" and go to "Faisal's" and "Khalil's" instead. We played Arabic music and despised those who did not. In our self-conscious enthusiasm, it should be admitted, we also went to unnecessary extremes.

In one meeting Samir came up with a novel proposition that we discussed with fascination and later approved unanimously. He claimed that here we were, sitting like a bunch of sons, wearing jeans and corduroys. "Why aren't we wearing our own national dress?" he demanded. "The ighal, the jellabiya? Why not?"

We listened, for his question seemed to be phrased rhetorically. "Do you remember that day in class?" he asked me, kicking his chair behind him and standing in the middle of the room. "Do you remember when you attacked Mr. King in class, because, you told him, he had been in the Middle East for ten years and he could not speak any Arabic? And do you remember in the course of the argument how he said that many of us did not show a great deal of respect for our own culture for we were in a such a son hurry to adopt his? Well, the son of a whore was right, I say. Why aren't we wearing our own national dress, for example, and wearing his instead?"

We debated that and a resolution was passed. Money would be collected and saved till we had enough to buy a jellabiya and an ighal each. The plan called for the eight of us to descend on the school the same day wearing our new Arab gear and, although it was conceded that we would elicit snickers and derision, we were to remain calm and above all explain why we were wearing it and that it was our own national dress of which we were proud. At any rate, it was all for the cause.

Three weeks later we bought the dresses and I took mine home and stood in front of the mirror to change.

"What the hell is this, fellow?" my father said. I thought for a minute he was going to give me that long talk about how my brother was working in the desert slaving his son guts out so that I could go to school and lead the cushy life I had been leading and how I was wasting my money on shit and my time on politics.

"This is our national dress, dad. You see, we are going . . . I am going to start wearing it from now on," I said. When he did not understand, I added lamely as an afterthought: "I am . . . I mean, we should be proud of it, you know. I intend to wear it around, you know, and to school."

My father looked at me as if I were crazy. He did not say anything.

"Is there any reason why I should not be wearing the ighal and jellabiya? They *are* our national dress," I said a trifle hesitantly. During the last meeting at the cell we had agreed on how firm we should be in our conviction that there was no reason to be ashamed of our heritage, no reason why we should not be embracing it. We were not to be swayed. We were to keep our cool when confronted by the predictable accusation of being exhibitionists.

"No, boy. There is absolutely no reason. I think it is an admirable idea," my father said. "Admirable, I say."

Then he did something strange which served to confirm my belief that I was not only doing the right thing, but doing a worthy thing. He left the room and came back a few minutes later with a hatta, a kind of checkered scarf usually worn under the ighal.

"Look, this used to belong to your Uncle Adnan. He died defending that same heritage you are trying to resurrect or perpetuate. You can wear it," he said. A Palestinian hatta; red, check-ered.

It was a bit too dramatic for me because I knew when Uncle Adnan was remembered around the house it was done with a hush. To us all (and no doubt to his wife and two daughters who stayed behind in Israel), he was a hero and a martyr, for he died in battle in 1947. And although in life he may have been no more than an ordinary fighter, in death he became a legendary figure, a brave man, a charismatic leader, and a great organizer. To have been given his hatta was an affirmation of my own struggle for identity and the correct direction I was taking for myself. I hun-gered for satisfaction that there was no shame in being a Palestin-ian, in my belief that not being a Lebanese, Syrian, American, Italian, Afghani, did not mean I was less than they were, or felt less, or hoped less, or lived my day less than they did.

I stood in front of the mirror and put the jellabiya on and ad-justed the hatta and ighal on my head. I walked around the room with the bottom of the jellabiya trailing behind me. There was a sudden rise in my pulse. I felt a deep sense of contentment satu-rating my being, a feeling almost sexual in its intensity and grat-ification. I was a Palestinian, an Arab, and no other man in the universe could wear this, would wear this, unless he was a Pales-tinian, an Arab, a man proud of his identity and self.

The fad caught on at school; it caught on at the American Uni-versity and around Ras Beirut among the student community. After a while the dress became accepted, and all students, at one time or another, wore it. It was a kind of proclamation, an adver-tisement of the fact that you were an Arab Nationalist, a Parti Syrien member, or just a person who was proud of his Arabism. The only group who continued to poke fun at the fad were the Fa-langists. "O, la, la," they would say in French, "C'est drôle, c'est bien drôle!"

It would not have been so bad if the sons had said that in Ara-bic instead of French.

Once our coordinator got picked up by the police and deported to Syria. This in itself would not have been so drastic if it were not for the background surrounding this man and the series of events that led to his arrest and deportation. Ibrahim Ouayni had been a coordinator for the Parti Syrien for roughly eight months before he was taken away. He was a Syrian lad of twenty-three who had studied medicine at the University of Damascus where he originally got into trouble with the authorities. Although he knew well that the campus was full of police informers, he continuously sounded off and organized small, quiet, anti-Nasser rallies. Predictably enough, he (along with a few other agitators) was carted off to jail where he stayed for seven weeks and where he was subjected to beatings and long sessions of interrogation. He was released with a warning to lay off active politics. He did not. He was picked up again and this time the last jail he had visited seemed like the land of milk and honey. He was placed in a damp cell and isolated from contact with the outside world (including his wife, whom he had married only six months before). He was later removed to another, better cell that he shared with three other political prisoners. Here, however, he found that he was being taken upstairs for a regular nightly session of questioning, the sole purpose of which was to break him completely rather than extract any useful information from him. The interrogators succeeded, for when he was released he discovered that he could no longer concentrate on his studies, perform simple tasks around the house, or make simple decisions. He left Syria and came to Beirut with his wife and stayed for a few months. When he felt better, he returned to Damascus (although not to the university), only to be picked up again. This time it was done presumably on orders from the Deuxième Bureau which wanted all anti-Nasser elements locked up on the eve of the Egyptian-Syrian union. He was taken to what was apparently a minimum security jail, for he managed to escape and illegally cross the Syrian border into Lebanon. He stayed with friends in Beirut, feeling safe, as he never registered with the police who thus had no record or trace of his whereabouts.

In the meantime he made a living doing translation work for publishers and teaching occasionally at private schools that were not sticklers for work permits. He led a semi-clandestine life but he seemed happy. Indeed, it was awesome that a man who had endured so much could have such staggering reserves of energy and enthusiasm and such humor and love in him. He would come to Samir's room for our weekly cell meetings and sit there with the contented look of a Buddha, interjecting an amusing observation here and there. Only when we talked about Syria, or the Syrian security police, would his face take on a look of panic. He would squint at the speaker, his eyes tightened into two slits, and appear demonstrably perturbed. He still had not recovered enough from his ordeal to let associative words go over his head. His only fear was to be caught and returned to the hands of the Deuxième Bureau.

He was making plans to have his wife come to Beirut to be with him and some of the boys at the Parti were helping him. Contact was made with her and she was quietly arranging to leave Damascus. Whether these activities themselves tipped off the police or whether there was an informer in the Parti, no one can say; but Ibrahim was picked up by the Lebanese sharmootas one night as he was playing the oud in his room. I do not know if it is true or not, but Samir claimed a few days later that Ibrahim had broken down completely as he was being arrested and shoved into a police van. He said that the Syrian had collapsed into a corner of the room and begged the sons not to have him sent back to Syria. He was sobbing and acting in a very strange manner. If all that is true, it still could not be held against him. Who knows what was going through the man's psyche as he was suddenly confronted by the knowledge that soon he would be back in a Syrian jail subjected to the same horrors that had nearly robbed him of his sanity and that he feared so much. At any rate, there was nothing we at the cell could do, although of course the Parti was going to do its best to help get him out.

On weekends Samir used to work downtown in the Borj, setting up a small stall of trinkets (razor blades, cheap lighters, pens, etc.) in front of any closed shop in the area. Business was never brisk, but what he made was enough to supplement the grant he had been offered, and came in handy for the occasional trip he took to Baalbek to visit his parents at the camp. As he had no license to peddle, he was always on the lookout for police vans or individual cops, which made life miserable for him. From time to time we used to go down to the Borj to keep an eye on traffic and case the street for over-enthusiastic gendarmes, thus enabling him to do his work. He used to have his goods spread out on a tablecloth on the ground and, with the word from any of us about approaching ben sharmootas, he would quickly fold everything into a bundle and stand nonchalantly as if he were waiting for someone.

When things were quiet down the street, the group of us would sit down to talk or read or get into heated arguments over politics. Once Bilkassem, one of the boys from the cell, bought a small bottle of arak and became nearly paralyzed after drinking it neat. He stood up to give a speech and attracted quite a few passers-by who listened to his diatribe on issues that ranged from the guerrilla war in Algeria to the Falangist vermin. One man told him to shut up, and Bilkassem became violent.

"You want to fight, ben sharmoota? Come on, son. I'll take you on."

"Why don't you go back to where you came from, you Palestinian sons of whores who sold their land to the Jews!" This was a standard accusation to level against a Palestinian and over the years it became hackneyed.

The five of us (and two were Lebanese) walked over to the man and Samir told him to keep moving or he would break his neck. Things got more complicated when Bilkassem, who got off his soap box, started shouting "Let *me*, I'll break the son's neck. Okay, ben sharmoota, come here, I'll break your neck!" The higher Bilkassem's voice was raised and the more vociferous he became, the bigger the crowd got.

"Come on, ben sharmoota," Bilkassem persisted.

The man somehow managed to slip away and in his place two cops materialized, complete with truncheons, guns, and a three-day stubble.

"What's going on here?" one of them asked.

While we were trying to explain the problem we discovered Bilkassem had disappeared, drunk as he was, presumably to chase after the man who had insulted his people. The cops could not get a clear picture of what had been going on—we, along with the on-

lookers who were volunteering their own version of the story,
were all speaking at once—so they told us to move on.

Samir picked up his bundle and we hurried down the street to
find Bilkassem. As we neared the Roxy Cinema we noticed a small
crowd gathered outside. And there was Bilkassem, carrying on
about how the Palestinian people sold land to the Zionists at the
early stages, in good faith, but how no land was sold when it became obvious that the Zionists harbored nefarious intentions in
our homeland. Before we managed to drag him away, he again
challenged those in the crowd who were Falangists, reactionaries,
fascists, and those with right-wing tendencies, to come and fight.

"I'll take on any son, any ben sharmoota right now," he said.

"Let's go, boy," we told him.

"Any ben sharmoota. Right now, right now I say. Why should
we take khara from these sons. Right now. Now or never. There
are six of us."

We eventually got on the tram and the son carried on even
there; but as it was a Ras Beirut tram, heading for the American
University, most of the passengers were students so no problems
ensued. In fact, Bilkassem's antics elicited a great deal of sympathetic laughter and at times mock-serious applause.

Although the incident was in later days a source of amusement
for us, Bilkassem was severely censured at the cell for an act that
was considered highly unrevolutionary—so serious a group of
teenagers were we.

Another weekend at the Borj coincided with the visit the Sixth
Fleet was paying to Beirut, and the city was crowded with American sailors. Three of them stopped to have a word with us and
Samir went to pains to explain to them "our cause." They obviously did not follow, but they asked a few naive and polite questions and seemed highly impressed by Samir's command of their
language. Every time they changed the subject, to ask about a
good bar to drink in, Samir would steer the conversation back to
revolution, Zionism, Algeria, imperialism, and self-determination.
We took them up to "Khalil's" where we had ice cream and later
to the University where they watched a baseball game between
the American Community School and a team from the fleet. This

was where the three sailors explained at length the intricacies of the game and the significance of each move the players made. Samir was bored. Then they took us for a visit on their ship where we again talked.

At the cell Samir and Bilkassem complained that American sailors were not politically conscious and that it had been a waste trying to educate decadent bourgeois elements like that. I suggested the contact was interesting on the human level; Osama, the Lebanese boy, said the cause was not harmed; someone else interjected that we had had a good time.

And all this, for God's sake, actually went into the minutes of the 42nd meeting of the "Ittihad" cell of the Parti Syrien Nationaliste in the city of Beirut on May 12, 1957.

Shortly after that I graduated from high school and was granted a scholarship to study in England where I stayed for three and a half years.

3. Damascus and the Desert

I returned to the Middle East more embittered, more disillu-
sioned, more unhappy than when I left. There was a rage within
me. An anger. A hate. A fury that was almost animal in its intensity.

I had been cheated by the world, by the gods, and by history.
Knowing of the agonies of men from more devastated worlds, with
more crippling experiences, did not humble me. Knowing that
others had suffered more in the past in Nagasaki and gas chambers; that others were suffering more in the present in massacres
and wars in Africa and the East; that others will suffer more in the

future in India and elsewhere just at the pain of being, did not comfort me. The pain of others will touch the world within them. I cannot experience it for them. It cannot touch the essence within me as my own pain can. There was no room to align my aspirations with reality as I sensed it; to reconcile the promises with facts as I grasped them; to live in my homeland as I knew it.

I sit in a dank shaay shop and watch the faces in the street. I listen to the sounds of traffic and lottery ticket peddlers and men shouting. The rain falls. Does not the rain fall everywhere? Must the Gates of Eden be open to some, shut to others? How the men who have waited out the night want to see the advent of a new dawn!

Let me see your ID card, the cop says. I am just sitting in a shaay shop, drinking tea and thinking, what if I didn't have my ID card on me? I walk the streets along the Corniche. An old woman with beads stops me. An old face. Beautiful. Ironic. Wrinkled with crazy wisdom. A face I knew from the camps. She grabs my wrist gently and smiles, a smile divested of humor. She looks at me, into my eyes. She has a heap of embroidered shirts slung over her shoulder.

"Um Ismael, yirda alleik," I say with sudden recognition.

"Yirda alleik, ben," she says.

"God bless you too."

"How have you been?"

"I have just returned from England, I was studying there."

"I can't hear you," she tells me.

"I was studying in England, I came back a few days ago."

"Ah, yirda alleik."

Looking at her limp, frail body and listening to her words, spoken in a distant, weak voice, I know Um Ismael no longer utters those vociferous threats and obscenities of yore. Her resistance has been broken, her old defiance of the world, a world she had treated with contempt in those first years around the camp, has now succumbed under many weights. When did you and your generation of Palestinians die, Um Ismael, when were you defeated, when did the spirit of resignation slowly begin to creep into your souls? How? How was it? When was it that the Palestinian mind wrinkled with gloom and saw the whole world as the land of no man?

"Are you still at the camp?" I ask.

"Yes, ben, I am still there."

Swear, Um Ismael, swear woman. Say ben sharmoota on the camp, on the world, on the Zionists, on the two-bit Lebanese; say ben sharmoota on God; throw rocks and garbage at passing army trucks as you used to do, woman. Don't give up. We are becoming a defeated people, fading, descending. A piece of fluff blowing hither and thither in the air, disintegrating.

We talk for a few minutes and then she walks away, adjusting the colored, embroidered shirts over her shoulder. To peddle. I watch her for a long while. All the Ums and all the Abus, that other generation of Palestinians who are never going to recover, injecting themselves with despair instead of hope and resilience.

I now began to have thoughts about what kind of people we were, we have become, and I found I did not know. What kind of metamorphosis went through our psyches to bring about such changes in our outlook on reality? What about us, that other half of the Palestinian people, the newer generation? Are we cultivating the knowledge that we can ask the world if it is afraid of us? That we have not been defeated by it because we have retained our sanity and our existential perspective?

I hated. I hated the world and the order of reality around me. I hated being dispossessed of a nation and an identity. I hated being the victim of social and political Darwinism. I hated not being part of a culture. I hated being a hybrid, an outcast, and a zero. A problem. Dwelling in a world that suspended me aloft, petrified my being and denied me a place among men until the problem was resolved. A world where this problem and I became interchangeable. Where I, the problem, was ignored by some, rejected by others, and derided by the rest.

So I hated. And the world hated me because I hated. It was the circle, vicious and insane, that we lived in. I hated the world for hating me because I hated. A hate not of the self, for I still possessed my pride, intellect, and humanity, but one directed at the cruelty of the cosmos and its denizens.

I sat on the rocks and watched the men fishing. The waves broke quietly at my feet. I returned home through the back streets, down the busy shopping center, to the Place de Martyres, the main Emir Bashir Street, then through more back streets. I got home, walked up the stairs to the third floor, encountering kids with their bicycles and toys, and mothers with their washing. I opened the door of the apartment with my key and let myself in. My mother wants to know if there is any news of my work permit yet. I say no. She begins to bug me with questions about whether I will accept any kind of temporary job. A teaching job perhaps, she says, at a night school, where no work permit is required. I say no. How about calling on Mr. McMeekin, she asks, maybe he can help. I say no. Have I tried speaking to so and so? I say damn it, no. No.

My father is now dead. I am saddened by the loss of him. I sit in a room to read. I close the door. I have one sister at the American University. I have a brother working in the desert. I have a mother who wants to know why I am angry and why I am sad and why I am not hungry and whether I feel sick and why I won't eat my damn hommos, with olive oil, which is good for me.

I say I want to get out of Beirut because I am sickened by the place. She says go visit your Uncle Deeb in Damascus and when you come back your work permit will be ready. I say no. Ben sharmoota on my work permit. When I come back, I will apply for a job in the desert with Aramco. Then I will go away, far, wherever I can go, whichever country will grant me a visa to live. The whole Middle East is a sick lie. An abominable comedy. A repulsive quagmire. The area I saw from the outside when I lifted a stone, and looked. Let them shriek their holier-than-thou promises about Palestine. Let the whole world play games at my cost—at the UN, at the conference tables, at the Big Four or Big Forty meetings, at their commemoration days, and at their ben sharmoota help-the-refugees collection days.

Give me a gun, man, and I will blow my own or somebody else's brains out. Leave me alone, and I will go somewhere to hide behind the hills; maybe then I can begin to understand. And on the way I will write slogans on all the walls of all the shithouses

from here to Katmandu to tell the world what I think of their gods
and their angels, of their values and matrix of logic, of their sense
of history and the sadness of poetry suppressed in the soul of disinherited men. For that is where it all belongs. In the shithouse.

Before I left Beirut (getting a permit to cross the border into
Syria through a wasta, a kind of bureaucratic pimp who, for a fee,
will promptly get you your laissez-passer from the immigration department officials with whom he is in collusion), I severed my relations with the Parti Syrien Nationaliste and told them I was no
longer available for meetings or running a cell.

I took a service cab from downtown Beirut, with four other passengers, and looked forward to a respite from Lebanon and the
problem of a work permit. Syria was still the Northern Province of
the UAR but would secede in three months. My Uncle Deeb,
whom I had not seen for six years, was a man in his late forties
who was head of the Syrian Workers Union, and who had a year
before been sent as a union representative to the U.S.S.R., where
he was taken on an extensive tour of factories. I was anticipating
an interesting stay with him and hoping to draw him into a discus-
sion of the political problems in the region, although I had no ink-
ling of the ideological character of his ideas.

It was a hot day, but it became cooler as the cab moved up the
mountains of Lebanon, heading east. Next to me sat an arrogant
American lady of middle age who was squirming in her seat,
afraid of being touched by a native. When she eventually opened
her mouth, it transpired that she was doing missionary work for
Palestinian refugees in Jordan. She had none of the confirmed
goodness associated with a missionary's job—just a hard face and
a mouth that closed almost without lips. She had a moustache of
heavy fluff. I asked her how she was doing at the camps. She
sniffed contemptuously. "I do my job. We are all trying to help,
you know. But those people. They just *will not* help themselves.
They will not, you know. The way they are living, it is horrible. I
mean they refuse to help themselves. It's not our fault, you
know." I told her simply that she was a stupid bitch, and ignored
her the rest of the journey. I refused to answer any of her questions about how I dared, just how I dared.

In my frame of mind I was reduced to getting a cheap satisfaction from abusing a poor, embittered spinster on her way to Jordan to tell the refugees how they should love God, because she herself had no one else to love.

Damascus in those rare times when the country is not embroiled in political intrigue, is a charming city with a great many of its ancient buildings and souqs still intact. Its people have retained many of the gallantries of olden days and have refused to emulate, unlike the Beirutis, Western modes of behavior and taste, preferring instead the traditional ways of living. But Damascus when I visited, on the eve of Syria's secession from the UAR, was a tense horrifying city, with police checking on the activities of ordinary citizens, and ordinary citizens checking on other ordinary citizens; with a consequent distrust between neighbor and neighbor, friend and friend, colleague and colleague, employer and employed. The Deuxième Bureau, which was run by an Egyptian, had informants who permeated the very highest and the very lowest of all business hierarchies. Damascus, as I was to sense in my short stay, was indeed the police city par excellence, the epitome of fear from above and around, a city where paranoia reigned supreme.

My uncle picked me up at the terminal, and after handshakes and emotions, commented stiffly on my blazer which had my college badge on it. Take it off, he told me, they will think you are British or they will think you are pro-British. They are pretty suspicious here, he said. I did not know who "they" were, but I presume he meant everybody. He looked agitated and nervous.

As we walked down the busy streets, I pointed out to him that there were pictures of Nasser hanging in the windows of practically every shop. "Let's not talk politics in the street," he said conspiratorially and *sotto voce*. "It's not a good idea."

I was beginning to think maybe I should not have left Beirut.

When we got home, my aunt, who was my mother's sister, burst into tears and mumbled about how I was a little boy, yes that high, only that high, when she last saw me. And now, look at me now, a big boy. A man. With a good education too. I was going to be as obedient and good a son as my brother, wasn't I? And when we soon go back to our homeland, I'll do even better there. I knew, of course, she said, that because she had no sons or daughters of her own we were all hers too, to love and cuddle. Don't I remember the time, she asked, when I must have been just that high, remember, when I got my first suit cut to measure at the tailor's, Abu Sami's, remember, and I cried because it was not ready when he said it would be? And what about your sister, how is she doing at the University, hey, heard she was getting good marks, your mother says, and tell me about your brother. Now tell me, when is his wife expecting, hey, you know for sure? He wants a son of course, doesn't he, hey? When this whole spiel was over and I had eaten beyond my ordinary capacities, I sat and had a long talk with my uncle.

At that time Syria, or the Northern Province, was engaged in a war of impassioned rhetoric with Jordan. Radio Amman hurled abuse and accusations of betrayal of the cause, with Radio Damascus, never to be outdone, hurling back fresh abuse and accusations. Loyal Syrians were not of course expected to tune in on Radio Amman to listen to the lies from those lackeys, if for no reason other than that they did not know if the volume on their set was low enough. My aunt was now fiddling with the knobs and accidentally received Amman's commentator as he was finishing a sentence: ". . . the prison. The walls of the prison that is your country, occupied by ruthless Egyptians and Syrian traitors. Rise Syrians; rise and throw the shackles . . ."

My uncle said frantically: "Turn that thing off, or down, for God's sake, woman!"

I was incredulous at all this and asked him if the police did in fact do anything when someone was overheard listening to Radio Amman. He said no, but they filed his name and kept an eye on him. Occasional harassment was usual. He seemed to believe that the union with Egypt would not last much longer, as the tension was becoming unbearable, and that that was probably why the police had intensified their repression.

"I trust you, my boy," he said.

I replied that I did not for one moment expect him not to trust me. He looked at me sadly and sheepishly, rubbed his eyes for a long while, and said he was sorry, but living in Syria under those conditions did not help. "But I think that Nasser is the most insincere leader the Arab world has ever had, and this is a world, mind you, full of insincere leaders," he said.

I told him I had similar views. We talked about how the Egyptians should never have had to involve themselves in the affairs of the Levantine countries, as traditionally they were Egyptians first and foremost, only vaguely associating themselves with us in the past; and about his trip to Russia; and about the dormant Palestinian issue. But he seemed reluctant for the moment to discuss his job with the Syrian Workers Union.

"I feel I am going to burst wide open," he said. "I can't talk to anyone. Trust anyone. It's unbearable."

In the evening we went to a cafe in the city where we sat for two hours and talked about mundane matters—he had warned me not to allude to anything political. He ordered a narjeel, and when it arrived he suddenly asked me, as if he had just remembered, whether I wanted one too. I said fine. I had smoked only one before, learning to suck gingerly at the pipe, drawing smoke from the tip which had a lump of strong tobacco on it, lit by a piece of burning coal. The tobacco plant, although close to the family cannabis, has a much milder and lighter effect on the brain. After a while the sound of the water gurgling in the narjeel becomes pleasant and soothing. You feel a glow around you and a warmth within you. It was becalming, sitting there in a side-street cafe, suddenly feeling afloat, elevated, restful on a cushion of air, watching the crowd saunter along, listening to the cries of the muazzens from the mosque, in a city that was no longer menacing.

The next day my uncle took me around to see some factories where I was introduced to the local union representatives and had coffee with the foremen and supervisors. These put on a show of ultra friendliness, slapping me on the back, welcoming me heartily, and going to lunatic extremes to point out how efficient their personnel were. I noticed there were a lot of Egyptian workers around—short, undernourished, and illiterate fellaheen, some of the hordes who had swarmed into Syria following the union to find employment and a better standard of living.

When we left, my uncle said matter-of-factly: "They don't believe you're my nephew; they think you're from the government
or the police."

"Oh, come on!"

"I know these people. I know their reactions. They were afraid.
They were crawling."

I told him that he was a union man and that surely they would
not believe he was in collusion with the police.

"Maybe, son. Maybe."

At a small glass factory that was owned and managed by a short
bald-headed Syrian, I was shown some of the exquisitely done
work while my uncle and the manager were talking in the office.
The man who took me around was a middle-aged Egyptian in a
brown overall who spoke condescendingly of the effort put in by
the Syrian staff, explaining that he had to be on their backs all the
time or otherwise production would fall. Every now and again he
stood by some poor fellow to shout abuse at him and threaten him
with dire punishment unless he stopped fooling; or he would give
orders to someone, raising his voice with contempt when the
order was queried. Then he would turn to me, smiling broadly, his
voice a hush, and lead the way reverentially.

He was a most obnoxious creature.

Back in the office, drinking coffee and exchanging polite pleasantries with my uncle and Abu Omar, the manager, I discovered
from a remark my uncle made that Abu Omar had a son studying
in England. I expressed interest, saying that I had been there myself, and asked him what university his son was studying at.

"Oh well, I am not sure I know. You see, he hasn't been there
for a long time," Abu Omar said, looking at me tensely. Then he
changed the subject and started talking about the rewards that
await a holidaymaker in the Cedars of Lebanon. I did not realize
until later that the poor paranoid man, thinking I was connected
with the Deuxième Bureau, was afraid his son would be in some
kind of danger if he revealed his whereabouts.

On my last night in Damascus, my uncle, sitting with me in his
study, told me what his trouble was. He said that three of the top
men at the Syrian Workers Union were in jail, on no specific

charges, and a fourth had been released and subjected to beatings and torture. Soon after that, my uncle and the remaining men on the Board signed a secret petition condemning that action against their union colleagues and had one man take it to Cairo and hand it to Nasser personally. But the man, along with his document, was stopped at the airport by security police and taken into custody, somewhere in Damascus, although no one yet knew where. As the meeting which resulted in the decision to sign the petition was presumably secret, and as all the members had decried police intervention in their affairs and the arrest of their men, agreeing unanimously that action be taken to stop it, it was obvious they had a Deuxième Bureau plant in their midst who must have informed his superiors of these goings on.

My uncle spoke quietly, pondering the flame of his cigarette, as if addressing himself. "I don't know what is going to happen now. All this took place last week. But I am quite certain we are going to be hearing from our sinister friend, Colonel Sarraj, very soon."

Before I left the following day, I promised myself either to get drunk or smoke a narjeel upon arriving in Beirut.

In Beirut, I had to register my return to Lebanon with the police. I had also reported to the Damascus police upon arrival and departure, producing two photographs each time. When it comes to travel, the lot of a refugee is not a pleasant one. Very often what a stateless person, from any part of the world, dreams of, hungers for, is possession of a valid passport. The indignities and harrowing obstacles that accompany a stateless travel document are infinite and can never be conveyed to other mortals. You feel robbed of a dear and wonderful thing that other men take for granted: the freedom to travel to a place you want to visit; the ability to go on a whim, when your fancy takes you, to a country, a town, a spot, a locale in this big world; you yearn for that little book, with your picture, telling all those whom it may concern to allow the bearer to pass freely without hindrance, and to assist him or her by affording him or her the protection he or she may need. Well, I needed that like I had never needed any other thing in my life. The simple privilege of passing freely without hindrance in other parts of the world; the simple right, like privacy and love-making and watching a sunset and going to bed early and writing a bad poem and drinking strong tea, that other men acquire by birth.

I went to the Zeitoony looking for a modest bar to get drunk in; it took some time to find one, as I had a great distaste for those air-conditioned ones that were pervasive in Beirut, with glossy counters and foreign "artistes" (so the barmaids called themselves). I spotted one near the wharf, with a neon-lit Shell sign blinking weakly behind it. The letter S was blacked out. I walked in and drank cheap arak for four hours. I walked out, saluted the sign, and went home, talking to myself on the way.

It took four weeks to get on the plane to Saudi Arabia. Aramco is a thorough company. Three interviews. Two medical checkups. A private detective to check one's background and activities. An intelligence test. A trade test. Forms to sign. More forms to sign. They even get your stateless travel document from the Aliens' Section. They have a full-time wasta on their payroll.

Then the plane landed at Dhahran airport in the middle of the afternoon on a summer day. This was the desert. This was veritable heat. Heat that blinds. Sweat escapes from the skin to wash down over the body in little jerky rivulets. The nerves are frayed. Sudden fatigue benumbs you. You curse the customs men between wet lips, but finding no alcohol, they let you go.

Soon you are in an air-conditioned office, frightened of the nightmare that is outside. I was made to wait until the evening to beat the heat, then driven to Ras at Tannura where I was to begin work at the Industrial Training Center as a teacher of English. The Saudi driver says to me: "Salam alleik, ben."

"Wa alleik el salam," I say. I am fascinated by his long white robe and little knitted hat.

"And how is the good person of your father?" he wants to know.

"He is doing fine."

"And the person of your respected grandfather?"

"He is good."

"And I trust the rest of your good family are in excellent health."

"That they are. I thank the Lord."

"Blessings," he says.

"Blessings," I say.

He ushers me, an American, and three Saudis into a red van and drives off along bitumen through the desert. Two miles out of Dhahran the sands overwhelm the senses in their indestructible infinity. From time to time, in the distance, a hydroformer is spitting fire into the sky, dwarfed by the setting sun and the enormity of the land. Apart from these pockmarks, nothing is to be found, nothing lurks on the face of the desert, behind the dunes, across the horizon.

Two hours later the bus stops near a huge power line and the Saudis get out to pray. They go through the rituals of ablution using sand in the absence of water and begin to follow the movements of the Immam in kneeling, folding their arms, and kissing the earth. In front of them the base of the tower stands like a gigantic monster, alien and not of the desert, its spreading legs of steel rising over the men. They are like gnomes at its feet, their activities so strangely unconnected to its functions. Here, in fierce confrontation, in irreconcilable conflict, is the meeting of two worlds, two realities, two dialectics intruding upon each other in the expanse of the desert. The one abstract and in harmony with, the other exact and in violation of, its essence.

The American is sitting next to me. He is holding onto a bag and a safety hat. He says: "And how are you, boy?"

"Marhaba," I say, and hope he knows idiomatic Arabic and the "tu" form. He does not.

"Where you from?"

"From Haifa."

"Fucking good place," he says. If my eyes were daggers, he would be viciously stabbed to death.

"Where *you* from?" I ask.

"Baton Rouge; that's in . . ."

"Ah, mahal ben sharmoota."

"What?"

"Mahal ben sharmoota."

"What's that again?"

"Mahal ben sharmoota," I intone.

"Is that Arabic for something?"

"Yes."

"Ya?"

"Fucking good place."

"What is?"

"Baton Rouge."

"Hey, did you learn English in the States?"

"No, did *you?*"

I would be viciously stabbed to death if his eyes are daggers; consequently a breakdown in communications ensues. We are quiet the rest of the journey. Except once he offers me a Lucky Strike and I say in Arabic I prefer my own, his brand is too harsh.

There are over ten thousand middle Americans working in Saudi Arabia for the Arabian American Oil Company (Aramco), in its three centers around the Persian Gulf, Dhahran, Ras at Tannura and Abqaiq. Three transplanted American towns with air-conditioned houses, front yards, back yards, rotary clothes driers, supermarkets, newsstands, golf courses (for winter games), churches, schools, theaters, and cute babies with freckles on their noses and mothers with curlers.

Aramco, the most paternal company in the world, in an effort to keep a high retention ratio of its staff, will go to extremes to make those who work for it, especially if they are Americans recruited in the United States, very happy. Its employees get free houses, free transportation from and to the States for their wives and kids and furniture and dogs; it supplies houseboys, pays phenomenal salaries and, through its purchasing officer in the Hague, regularly supplies the three centers with frozen food, paperbacks of Harold Robbins, the *Daily News,* and tennis balls. If Aramco employees from the U.S. can put up with those times in the summer months when they are out of their air-conditioned offices or homes, then life for them in Saudi Arabia can be very comfortable. Some families, whose sons and daughters are at colleges in the U.S. or at the

American Community School in Beirut, have been living there for many years, waiting for the opportune moment in their early fifties to retire to a spot in the world of their own choosing.

In recent years, the Saudi government has applied pressure on Aramco to hire and train as many Saudis as possible, with the aim of ultimately replacing foreign (non-Arab) staff. But the Saudi workers, a great proportion of whom were illiterate and as a result unsuited to hold even the most modest positions, were seen as a problem—a problem made additionally complex as the government wished to see its nationals in a position to take over the future running of the company, but not at the cost of eradicating illiteracy in their midst. For reasons that the royal family and Aramco's high echelons understood well, an appreciable increase in the literacy rate of the Saudi people was to be avoided. The company then proposed, as a half measure, to open special schools, Industrial Training Centers, to coach their local personnel in the fundamentals of reading, math, English, and science. The students were given time off work to attend classes and lectures. The stipulation was that there were to be no studies offered in the arts and no mention of or allusions to politics, world current events, or the forbidden apple, unionism. (There was one case of a teacher who was reported to have discussed with his students the concept of the term "strike," which presumably occurred in a textbook he was teaching. He found himself the following morning at Dhahran airport awaiting the first available flight out of the country.)

You were allowed to brew your own grog in your back yard and even sell it to friends, so long as you were "American" about it; you were allowed to deride and curse the local laws and the king, so long as you did it in the confines of your living room; you were even allowed to disregard the sensibilities and traditions of the nationals in your host country, so long as you did that within the area fenced in as your Center; but you were not allowed to discuss, teach, or otherwise introduce ideas having to do with history, politics, or unionism.

Only once did Aramco and the government find themselves, to

their utter surprise, faced by a strike observed enthusiastically by thousands of its non-American staff. This came about in 1954, soon after the initial influx of the Palestinians who were then being recruited in huge numbers by the company. The strike, a great success only insofar as it focused attention on the unfair share the Saudi people received in the allocation of funds from oil revenues (Aramco was paying the government, i.e., the king and his family, over $250 million in royalties during 1954 alone), lasted for three days and achieved no positive benefits or concessions for any of the workers. Soon after that the police forced the Saudis to return to work, using sticks to beat them; 163 Palestinians were dismissed instantly and flown back home and the Saudi leaders of the strike were picked up and put in jail to receive daily floggings.° There have been no strikes since, and the employment requirements for Palestinians have become more stringent, reflecting the belief that they were culpable.

Two days after I arrived in Ras at Tannura, the fasting month of Ramadan started. For thirty days all Moslems, regardless of their nationalities, were to observe the fast from sunrise to sunset. In the medieval society of Saudi Arabia this law was taken very seriously indeed. It would have been inconceivable for a Moslem Arab to allow himself to be seen smoking, drinking, or eating by friend or foe—or the authorities, who were authorized to arrest anyone cheating on the fast and subject him to flogging or other similar types of punishment. There were men employed by the re-

---

° In a monograph titled *Desert Enterprise: The Middle East Oil Industry in Its Local Environment*, sponsored by the Center for Middle Eastern Studies and published by Harvard University Press in 1958, David Finnie attempts to delineate the gravity with which labor troubles were viewed by oil producing companies, and at the same time unwittingly underscores the minimal rewards the local workers shared in the oil profits (p. 102): "Loss of one day's production from a major producer like KOC or Aramco might cost something over a million dollars. A week of idleness per year would probably be more expensive than doubling the wages of all local employees." He adds: "The instigators of the Aramco strike in the fall of 1953 were arrested and severely punished—much more severely, indeed, than Aramco officials themselves would have preferred." He failed to mention that it was the company itself that instigated the brutal hunt for "instigators."

ligious hierarchy who walked the streets carrying sticks with which they herded the locals into the mosques at prayer times and insured that the ethics of Ramadan were adhered to.

With measures as repressive as these imposed upon the population, religion over the years became a synthetic and artificial round of mechanical rituals indulged in in the manner of morning ablutions and defecation. Faith was nonexistent. Belief was an accumulation of superstitions. The precepts of Islam as practiced by the Saudis in that region of the country were far removed from and alien to the spirit of the Koran they purported to follow. The men of God who ran the mosques and, in the old tradition of Arabia, the courts, were at best semi-literate.

My employment with Aramco lasted for one week and no more, before I was ignominiously kicked out and put on a plane.

I reported for work at the Industrial Training Center on my second day, the third day of Ramadan, and was ushered into the office of the principal, a middle-aged American called Henry Papas.

"Call me Hank," he said.

"Hello, Hank," I said uncomfortably.

"Well now," he said, washing his hands with invisible soap. "Tell me something about yourself."

I was beginning to feel very awkward. The joviality he was infusing between us was a put on.

"Well, well! Where did you learn to speak such faultless English?" he said after a while.

"I majored in it."

"Well, that's just wonderful, isn't it? Just wonderful." Even his accent was beginning to bug me.

He asked if I was satisfied with the accommodation that had been given me by the Housing Department. I said it was fine. In each of its three centers around the Gulf, Aramco had one camp almost exclusively for its Saudi artisan staff, another for skilled Saudis and for Palestinians who possessed no university degrees, and a third for Americans and for non-Americans who were professionals or graduates—but there were no American artisans or nonprofessionals living in the Arab camps. The camps were known respectively as Junior, Intermediate, and Senior, and there was an ascending level of comforts and facilities, with the Senior camp usually referred to as the American City. With all the care that went into creating a transplanted little American town, with air-conditioned houses and gadgetries, the name was apt.

A little American town, with little American people who did not want to share their toilets with the natives. With non-Americans.

I was handed a set of keys. The male secretary, Abu Kamil, a bald-headed Palestinian in his fifties who was always laughing about something, explained what each key was for. Desk, locker, library, classroom, toilet.

"A key for the toilet?" I asked.

"Yes, the toilets down the hall."

"Why are the toilets locked?"

"Well, there is one for the Arab staff and one for the American."

I was stunned. "What are you talking about, damn it, man?"

"The toilets are segregated here."

I felt like a drink of water, but I could not use the cold water fountain outside the reception office. It was Ramadan and the bastard sun had not yet set. I went into a laboratory where there was a tap, closed the door, and gulped down two glasses. My whole being was shaking with rage and mortification. I lit a cigarette. Someone walked into the room. The science teacher from Kansas, who, I had heard, had been a telephone operator before he was hired by Aramco, walked in and flashed me a great smile.

"Hello there," he sang.

I did not reply. He said something pleasant and meaningless, apparently to start a conversation.

I turned around. "Listen, fellow. I don't know you. I don't want to know you. Don't speak to me. I won't speak to you. Let's keep it that way."

During the day I spoke individually to the half-dozen or so Palestinian teachers, denouncing the blatancy of the segregated toilets. Not toilets for Intermediate staff and others for Senior staff; not toilets for ladies and others for gentlemen; but toilets for

Arabs and others for Americans. How could you take that, I pleaded. For God's sake, why have you made no attempts to resist it, condemn it, protest it? But they were mostly middle-aged men who had families to support back home, and sons and daughters, or brothers and sisters, to send to school, and did not want any trouble.

I waited for three days, until I could not take it any longer. I decided to bring the matter up at the staff meeting, which was held in the library. I expected to confront Papas with the demand for an explanation and challenge him to give reasons why this indignity should not be dispensed with. I was going to be calm and reasonable, even pleasant. But I had been working myself into an insane state of anger that morning, which was not helped by the ludicrous social dictates of Ramadan. If you want to smoke, you lock yourself up in your classroom; to drink, you sneak into the laboratory; to eat, you sit fitfully in the staff room. And always the dopey, self-satisfied, pimply-faced, middle-class, middle-aged, middle-American motherfuckers walking to and fro flashing you elastic smiles like they have nothing more important in their crew-cut heads than their tennis game or their next leave.

So when the meeting started, and before the principal even asked the secretary to read the minutes from the last week, I was on my feet. But I was not calm. I was not cool headed.

"Mr. Papas, I wish to ask you for an explanation. I demand an explanation from you, as to why you think it is necessary to segregate the toilets on the premises of this school in a manner that demonstrates such contempt and disrespect for the sensibilities of the non-American members of the teaching staff?"

"I understand," he said, taken aback. "Do you mind if we discuss that at the end of the meeting?"

"No, now!" I shouted. Something in me had snapped. Snapped suddenly, uncontrollably. "No, right now! Now. I want an explanation now," I shrieked. I kicked the chair behind me, and it fell on the floor. I walked out of the room and headed for the American toilet and kicked at it with my foot repeatedly and violently, shouting obscenities in Arabic and English. The lock broke and I walked in and opened my fly, intending to piss on the floor, the seat, and the walls; try as hard as I could, in my excitement I was not able to piss. Not a drop.

But I gave them my message and they in turn gave me theirs—the first flight out of the country. All the anger within me had seeped out. I sat back in the waiting room at Dhahran airport and waited for my flight. I even smiled smugly, and I spoke at length to a young American from the air force who worked on the base. He was about my age and we passed a relaxed hour together. I felt no need to show him the contempt I reserved for my encounters with Americans. We seemed to relate to each other, to respond with laughter or sadness about the same things.

"Maybe you will come to San Francisco one day," he said, giving me his address. "You can look me up. I am being discharged soon."

"If I do, I'll surely look you up."

I put the little piece of paper in my pocket and said good-bye. A name and an address; a little sharing of your humanity with another being that you recall and reflect upon at another time. A piece of paper you find again. A person who gave you testimony that he felt the same existential vibrations you did. A part of him. A symbol. A union. And you smile, feeling the inherent goodness and timelessness of the truth that you had just glimpsed.

I got on the plane. Nothing mattered to me any more. I hated not only Americans, not only Arabs, not only the Middle East, not only the whole world; I just hated. I was blind. I hated fiercely. I hated from within me and from outside of me. I was going nowhere. I was searching for a place where men were happy together. The Arabs cheated me, the Western world ignored me, the gods tormented me, and I turn twenty-two and sit on a plane heading somewhere, taking me to a place to get me away from another. I will start with Europe. Germany.

I get off the plane at Frankfurt. I have no visa. Only my stateless travel document.

"You have no visa. You can't enter the country," I am told by the immigration officer. "You are stateless; a visa is necessary."

Help me, man, ignore my little document of disgrace. You go back to Saudi Arabia, he says. Fuck you, I say. I don't care where you send me. Send me to heaven. I have been to hell already. Let me write you a little epic poem about it.

They tell me to wait while they examine my papers. I sit next to two nuns. They smile at me. I am reading a funny book by James Thurber about his problems with the *New Yorker*. I am smiling too. The official comes back and says I should go to England. I was there once before for a long time, he says, so they would let me in. I could go to the German embassy there and get a visa.

"Then you could come back," he says to me.

"Ben sharmoota," I say to him.

I fly to London and fly back without leaving the airport. A piece of paper is stapled to my passport saying that the holder of that document, who is "of dubious nationality," was refused permit to enter Her Majesty's realm. Her Majesty's realm did not need a permit, though, when it entered mine and robbed me of my nationality. But then there are those who need permits and those who do not. I did. And I was only asking for a permit to live in peace. I needed one, others did not.

I get off at Frankfurt airport again and continue reading Thurber. I laugh at the amusing parts in the book. I am sitting next to two young Americans with beards and rucksacks.

"How far you going?" I ask.

"India and Nepal."

"No kidding!"

"No."

"Good there?"

"Yes. You can live on an ashram. In the mountains. In Goa. In Katmandu. You can learn. Unlearn. You could be free. Happy."

"I could?"

"Yes. How far are *you* going?"

"I don't know. Maybe there too."

The Germans put me on a plane and fly me back to Beirut. I go through customs and the official stamps my passport and throws it in my face. A Palestinian should not have the temerity to travel. Or maybe I should have been at the end of the queue, not with all the other passengers. They might pick up my disease. My sickness. The only people who smile with me, who smile at me, are nuns and bearded Americans going to India and a youngster from San Francisco waiting to be discharged so he can go home.

I am met by a pugnacious Lebanese representative from Luft-hansa who wants me to sign papers certifying that I owe his company plane fares from Frankfurt to London, London to Frankfurt, Frankfurt to Beirut. I sign. All I want is to go home and sleep for three days. When will you pay us back, he wants to know.

One day soon, you motherfuckers, I'll pay you all back; all of us will pay all of you back. And it won't be long now. We won't be taking it on the chin for very much longer.

I get home and my mother wants to feed me—falafel and beans with tomato sauce and hommos with olive oil, which is good for me, she says. I go to sleep. Next day I make plans to leave. I work on getting visas. I walk the streets. I get the shakes. I go to the American University and meet old friends and sit under a tree. They still look to Nasser. They still run cells for the Parti. They still wait for Godot. They are still listening to Ahmed Said from Voice of the Arabs or uttering simplistic slogans of Levantine na-tionalism. I cannot wait to get out. I am being smothered by hate and frustration and sadness. Young Palestinians graduating from the University or returning from abroad with their degrees go in hordes to Arabia or Kuwait or other oil-rich states for employ-ment. Others hang around outside the campus unable to articulate their suppressed fury or translate it into constructive action.

My fury is becoming murderous as I wait for visas and sit by the Corniche writing bad poetry about how I hate the Arabs. I give private lessons. Lebanese students get charged the earth. I go to homes where I teach Palestinian kids how to analyze a sentence into clauses and what Hamlet's soliloquy was all about. Their mothers want to feed me hommos with olive oil, which is good for me, and I happily receive nominal pay. The Palestinians. We smile together. We share together.

I am in a service cab on my way from giving a lesson. I am tired. Restless. At a roadblock cops looking for an escaped crimi-nal stop the cab and ask for ID cards. I have not got mine. I break into a cold sweat; but today they seem in a good mood and they let me go with a warning. The driver says to me, softly, as if imparting a great advice to my good: "You people should know better than to walk around without your ID cards, you know; even Lebanese sometimes get in trouble for that."

"You people" he says to me, the ben sharmoota.

Two Falangists are sitting next to me, speaking French to each other. French, for God's sake. "Espèce de Palestinnien," one says to the other.

I flare up. I lean over and grab him by the collar. The cab stops and we struggle out. I get into a fist fight. I am like an animal. I challenge the passengers, the onlookers, the whole world to come near me and fight.

I get picked up and taken to the Borj police station.

"Lock this Palestinian up," one son says to another. Not "this man," "this trouble-maker," "this offender," "this bastard," "this law-breaker," but "this Palestinian." But they released me two days later. Charges dropped.

A Palestinian. Who knows what that is? I want to get away to understand.

I travel overland to the East and I live in India and Nepal. I stay in communes and ashrams and the streets and I get some peace. Peace, a kind of freedom from the known. For three years.

What are the problems of a Palestinian anyhow, in these lands that know the ultimate cosmos in pain and suffering; where men perish from hunger before the advent of a new day, and sleep in alleys where dogs die and dreams are never born?

4. The Guerrillas

Israel was the house the West built in the Middle East and to which it transplanted a group of people to impose on the region, in the tradition of a colonial diktat. This reality, despite its harshness, did not in fact touch the lives of the Arab masses or their world. They had lost no territory to the enemy, nor were their cities and land devastated by the ravages of war. But, smitten by defeat and continued frustration with an enemy which was every day becoming more entrenched in their midst, their indignation was projected in a torrent of incoherencies about their future "battle of destiny" and the dire fate awaiting the usurpers of the land of their Palestinian brethren. Mentioned repeatedly in their leaders' impassioned rhetoric, and identified as the final horror left in the wake of the colonial oppressor, the repugnant presence of Israel and its ultimate removal became, not a goal adopted within the rational framework of their policy planning, but a state of mind. That state of mind enabled the average Arab to believe firmly that his armies were indeed capable of driving the Jews into the sea and destroying that colonial diktat.

As the years passed, the enemy that was to be crushed and the grievance that was to be removed became increasingly abstract. To the men and women who lived in the northern regions of Syria, who populated the towns and villages of Iraq, who daily struggled against poverty and disease in Egypt, Israel and the Israelis, Zionism and imperialism were blurred concepts of no significance in the matrix of their lives. Even to those masses in the Levantine whose land abutted the enemy's and who were repeatedly reminded of his presence, the future "battle of destiny" was less real and feasible than the endeavors and vicissitudes of their nascent bourgeois society.

But there was one group now living in the Arab world for whom the creation of Israel had a staggering effect on the dimensions of existence and to whom the "usurped homeland" and the "battle of destiny" was of the most crucial and concrete importance. The Palestinians were the people from whom everything was taken and nothing was heard. They were the people on whose behalf all the threats against the enemy were made, and on whose behalf war was to be waged. For surely the Arabs themselves had no score to settle with the Zionists, no territory to liberate, no property to retrieve. Like puppets on a string, the Palestinians and their cause were constantly used whenever masters of ceremony took to the stage to amuse the masses, to hear themselves speak, to gain prestige.

With the turn of the second decade of their diaspora, the Palestinians were at the dead end of history, like a petrified long-forgotten species about to emboss its distorted image on a stone, arrested for all time. Their problem was being overlooked by the fourteen Arab states and bypassed at the international negotia-

tions over the Middle East. When it appeared on the agenda of
the UN General Assembly, the members endorsed a further allot-
ment of aid to UNRWA for "Arab refugees," and moved on to
weightier issues that had nothing to do with the fractured soul of a
whole nation in exile. The dispute between Israel and its neigh-
bors was never acknowledged as stemming from the dispersion of
the Palestinians, nor were they acknowledged as a party to be
consulted, a nation-party with a national identity.

The leaders of Israel rejected earlier UN resolutions that called
for the return of the refugees to their homeland. They rejected the
idea that the "so-called Palestinian people" existed, that they had
any rightful claim to repatriation, and repeatedly insisted that
they were the Arabs' problem not theirs and thus should be absorbed in their host countries or in Australia, Canada, or South
America.

Growing up in refugee camps and elsewhere, Palestinian
youngsters, more educated and more versatile than their counterparts in the Middle East, felt estranged and helpless. But unlike
their elders, who were beginning to feel the mental and physical
rot of resignation, they were looking around for an outlet to their
suppressed fury. It must follow, if we are to apply sociological hy-
potheses in this instance, that the social, political, and intellectual
mobilization of Palestinian youth, coupled with its discontent and
alienation, was inevitably going to produce mounting pressures on
it to transform the distorted structure of the reality they saw
around them in the Arab world.

With the Six Day War leaving the Arab world and its society
disjointed and inchoate, these young Palestinians took the matter
into their own hands for the first time and forcefully asserted their
sense of rediscovery and rebirth. They took to the stage, as it
were, to shout to the world that they were the Palestinians, remember, who had been shoved aside for two decades, and who
were now, as the only group in the Middle East not tainted by the
stigma of military defeat, forming their own political and guerrilla
movement, unfettered by commitments to the established order
and independent of the Arab governments. A movement reflect-
ing the forgotten generation, the New Palestinians, who, as they

grew up in or around the camps, had groped and waited in the shadows.

It is very difficult to pinpoint the date and precise place or activity that may be taken to mark the birth of the Palestinian guerrilla movement. As far back as the early fifties, young men and women fumbled their way through political clubs, cells, and trained in light arms. Some talked aggressively of their frustrations and impatience; others discussed the injustice of having the cause of the Palestinian nation so inextricably and helplessly predicated upon inter-Arab feuds and Arab League meetings; still others may indeed have dreamed up plans for an effective means of finding an outlet for a Palestinian political expression. But this was never translated into action until some of these men and women went abroad to study and, away from the repressive Middle East, were able to see their problem suddenly stripped of its exploitative features. In fact, prior to 1967 some Arab governments—notably Syria, Iraq, and Egypt—attempted to give sustenance to various Palestinian national groups and supported the formation of some commando organizations. But these never operated independently, for they were merely instruments of these governments' policy maneuvers. In 1964, for example, those governments encouraged the formation of a Palestinian organization headed by the disreputable hothead Ahmed Shukeiry, a reactionary of the old school who was as skilled in verbal pyrotechnics as were his Egyptian friends behind their microphones.

The first clandestine organization that was a truly Palestinian expression, Al-Fatah, was initially formed in the early 1950's by three Palestinian students at Stuttgart University who were ostensibly lingering on in their graduate work while in fact they were organizing their movement and recruiting among Arab students— away from Jordan and the Arab world where overt activity aimed at politicizing the masses would have been blocked or hindered.

These three students had been active in organizations of the revolutionary Left and in the Arab Nationalist movement since their teens. During their undergraduate student days in Cairo and Beirut schools, they had had a thorough grounding in politics and had watched carefully as the Algerian liberation war against

French settlers slowly evolved. They had seen all around them the death of the old order and the emergence of a new one as colonialism and imperialism lost their grip and leaders like Nuri el-Said, Farouk, King Abdulla, and others who served imperialist aims in the Arab world were swept away.

One of these students, Yasser Arafat, had come to the conclusion that the problem of the Palestinian people had too long been Arabized and infused into the Arab-Israeli dispute, and never realistically delineated. He was convinced that the Palestinians should take the responsibility of deciding their own fate, fighting their own battles, and liberating their own homeland. He was aware that alone the Palestinians could not defeat Israel, but if operations in the form of guerrilla forays were to start, attention would focus on the plight of the Palestinian people and their presence noted by a world that had forgotten or ignored their existence.

While the citizens of established societies could air their grievances or assert their claims in their parliaments and other elected government bodies, the Palestinians had no access to any of that. Their only recourse was to take the law into their own hands. And if by attacking their enemy they invited him to retaliate on the soil of their host countries, the more repeated and more escalated this retaliation became, the better it was for the Palestinians. If this were to cause the tension to culminate in an all-out war between the Arabs and the Israelis, that also was one of the objectives aimed at by Yasser Arafat and his two friends.

These were Hani el-Hassan and Khalil el-Wazir. They too were groping for a cure for the illusions, deceptions, and obscurities that dehumanized their cause. The former had connections with the FLN—the Algerian guerrilla group—which promised help, in the form of arms and training, following their own independence from France. The founders, along with the few newly enlisted members, held long elaborate meetings on campus to agree on strategy, policy, and tactics for their projected organization. It was to be known as Harakat Tahreer Falasteen,° or Al-Fatah for short.

Chapters of Al-Fatah, and of other independent groups, were

° Front for the Liberation of Palestine.

established underground at universities in Europe and the Middle East, and their recruits sent to Algeria and elsewhere for training. Although some of these organizations commenced operations along the Israeli borders in the early 1960's (and may have by their activities aggravated the Israelis into massing their forces along the Syrian border, thereby precipitating the Six Day War), they did not emerge fully on the scene till after 1967.

In its early stages, the armed struggle of the Palestinian people had to operate in strict secrecy and under difficult conditions. The various Arab governments were hostile to an independent Palestinian political or military expression. This stemmed from their lack of readiness or willingness to confront Israel and their opposition to isolating the Palestinian problem from the Arab-Israeli conflict. The Palestinian masses, still awaiting a solution from Nasser and conditioned by Arab statesmen to impassioned rhetoric, remained passive. Consequently the resistance operated underground, without mass popular support, and was hindered from galvanizing the Palestinian population. Government authorities made it additionally difficult for Al-Fatah and other embryonic groups—such as Abtal el-Awada, Heroes of the Return, which was one of the nuclei of the future Popular Front for the Liberation of Palestine—by subjecting their leaders to harassment, arrest, and torture.° Jordanian police were wont to raid refugee camps and imprison Palestinian political activists with revolutionary leanings. But the movement, though forced to function as a foco and employ armed violence without any political mobilization of the masses, nevertheless continued to thrive and, as was its avowed aim, to bypass the Arab governments. Its first commando operation against Israel was announced on January 1, 1965.

As its recruits returned from training in Algeria, action against the Israeli border was intensified. For their part, the Israelis adopted a strategy of hitting directly at the Arab states to make them in turn strike at the Palestinians. But the guerrilla movement was not given its major boost until they were able to fill the void left by the military collapse of the Arab states in the Six Day War,

---

° The first guerrilla was killed in 1965 by a Jordanian soldier.

a war which served as a stunning testimonial that the Palestinians could no longer rely on others to solve their problems. Al-Fatah, as well as other small and relatively obscure organizations, was inundated with applications from young Palestinians who had nowhere else to go and knew there was nothing else to do.

The ultimate emergence of ten independent guerrilla groups should not be taken as a manifestation of disunity on the broad issues confronting the Palestinian people and their common struggle, but of differences in ideological orientation and tactics. In the various meetings that were sponsored by the Palestine Liberation Organization, the umbrella group that coordinated policy planning and maneuvers, there was no question of the leader of one group denouncing another in the manner of an Arab statesman attacking his fellow Arab. For the guerrilla movement, fragmented though it was, derived its inspiration from the same principles drawn up in its early stages. These stated that:

—Revolutionary violence is the only way in which the fatherland can be liberated.

—This violence must be exercised by the mass of the people.

—The aim of this revolutionary violence is to liquidate the Zionist identity in its political, economic, and military forms, from all the occupied land of Palestine.

—Revolutionary action must be independent of any control either by state or party.

—This revolutionary action will be of long duration.

—The revolution is Palestinian in its origin and Arab in its extension.

Al-Fatah, which emerged as the strongest and largest of the ten member groups, concentrated on operations inside Israel and Israeli-held territory and placed no emphasis on political pronouncements; its aim was to make Israel acknowledge the right of the Palestinian people to return to their homeland—a secular Palestine that would accommodate all Palestinians: Jews, Moslems, and Christians. The Israelis would have to learn and the world be reminded that unless the Palestinian people's cause was heard and their grievances rectified, then guerrilla warfare and resistance would continue and intensify.

The Popular Front for the Liberation of Palestine, another guerrilla group, possibly the most hyperactive and left wing of all, agreed in principle with Al-Fatah, but in addition felt the need to agitate both for revolutionary change in Palestinian society *and* for the overthrow of all reactionary regimes in the Arab world. Since the Palestinians alone, the PFLP felt, were at this stage unable to make Israel recognize their just claims, then the Arab world should be genuinely radicalized and turned into a dynamic, socialistically structured society that could effectively confront Israel and fight alongside the Palestinians, who would be the vanguard of the revolution.

The PFLP was founded by a 44-year-old Palestinian physician, George Habbash, who, shortly after the June war, was still running a clinic in Amman with a group of nuns. He worked as a pediatrician and his patients were mostly refugees from the nearby camps. He had graduated from the American University of Beirut where he acquired his Marxist-Leninist leanings and belief that socialism was the only cure for the economic and spiritual ills of the Middle East. It was during the last confrontation with Israel that his consciousness as a Palestinian finally made him give up medicine, his wife and two children, and leave the capital of Jordan to join the guerrillas.

He was later asked by a foreign correspondent what it was in him that produced such a metamorphosis, what made him give up his job of saving lives and become a guerrilla to destroy them. He explained it this way:

It was 1967 and the Israelis came to Lydda. I don't know how to explain this . . . what this still means for us not to have a home, not to have a nation, or anyone who cares . . . they forced us to flee. It is a picture that haunts me and that I'll never forget. Thirty thousand human beings, walking, weeping . . . screaming in terror . . . women with babies in their arms and children tugging at their skirts . . . and the Israeli soldiers pushing them on with their guns. Some people fell by the wayside, some never got up again. It was terrible. One thinks this is not life, this is not human. Once you have seen this, your heart and your brain are transformed.°

° Oriana Fallaci, *Life*, June 12, 1970.

Dr. Habbash turned his group into a disciplined and compact organization of 3,000 politically minded intellectuals who later became noted for their operations abroad. They pulled a number of spectacular coups, particularly in Europe where they attacked El-Al aircraft and were involved in shoot-outs with security police at various airports on the Continent. Their activities culminated in September 1970 when they hijacked, then blew up, four civilian aircraft and took their passengers as hostages. The rationale was that the enemy and his property are vulnerable to attack wherever they may be found (this applies not only to Israel but also to American imperialism and its interests overseas), and if this results in attracting headlines, all the better, for the world that has long ignored the Palestinians is to be reminded that they have not yet vanished.

This PFLP policy of attacking established governments, disrupting their commercial life, endangering the safety of their nationals, challenging them to release guerrillas in prison for previous terrorist acts, and showing contempt for the established order, did not endear them to the world. Editorials in the world press, and governments both in the Middle East and the West, generally condemned them. Public opinion turned against them and the image of the whole resistance movement suffered immensely. Habbash's response to all that was:

> Our blows are directed at the weak parts in the enemy's structure, to throw him into confusion . . . The operations of the Front demonstrate that the safety and life of any imprisoned member of the revolution is no less valuable than the safety or life of any Westerner, and that it will not permit Arab lands or Arabs to be considered as fair game for abuse . . . Has it been said that these operations expose the lives of innocent people to danger? In today's world no one is innocent, no one is neutral. A man is either with the oppressor or the oppressed. He who takes no interest in politics gives his blessing to the prevailing order . . .°

The intractable nature of the PFLP also landed it in trouble with the PLO, and on two occasions it was expelled from the or-

---

° Cited in Peter Snow and David Phillips, *Leila's Hijack War* (London: Pan Books, 1970).

ganization and from its 27-member Executive Committee for acts
that were deemed damaging to the Palestinian revolutionary
movement and inconsistent with accepted methods of furthering
its aims.

Other guerrilla groups, although just as audacious as the PFLP,
were not willing to match its peccadillos in foreign countries and
restricted their operations to the Israeli border.°

What soon gave the fedayeen stature in the Arab world and in-
spired confidence in their abilities was an incident along the Is-
raeli-Jordanian border on March 21, 1968, that involved a large
number of Israeli troops, supported by air cover, in an attack on
an Al-Fatah stronghold at Karameh, near the Allenby Bridge on
the River Jordan. The Israelis, long used to successful encounters
with conventional Arab armies, moved toward the area at night
with their tanks and armored vehicles. This was to be a major operation to give a decisive blow to the commandos and annihilate

---

° Before the civil war erupted in Jordan there were ten guerrilla groups in operation. The smaller ones were ultimately absorbed by Al-Fatah or disappeared altogether. These ten were:

1. Popular Liberation Front: 2,000 members, led by Zaid Haydar.

2. Popular Front for the Liberation of Palestine: 3,000 members, led by Dr.
George Habbash.

3. Democratic Popular Front for the Liberation of Palestine: 1,000 members,
led by Nayef Hawatmeh. This was a splinter group of the PFLP which espoused a
complete break with the old policies, some of which they felt still prevailed.

4. Front for the Liberation of Palestine: 500 members, led by Ahmed Jibreel.
Also a splinter group of the PFLP; it disagreed with the accent on revolution.

5. Action Organization for the Liberation of Palestine: 700 members, led by Dr.
Issam Sartawi. A pro-Egyptian offshoot of Al-Fatah.

6. Popular Struggle Front: 400 members, led by Bahjat Abu Gharbiya. This
group occasionally engaged in terrorism abroad.

7. Al-Fatah: 10,000 members, led by Yasser Arafat.

8. Palestine Arab Organization: 350 members. An offshoot of the PFLP.

9. Al-Saiqa: 7,000 members. Sponsored by the Syrian Baath Party.

10. Arab Liberation Front. Affiliated with the Baath Party (Iraqi faction). Its
members were often trained by and attached to the Iraqi Army in Jordan.

The Palestine Liberation Organization (PLO) coordinated policy planning for
the ten commando groups. It had a 27-member Central Committee formed on
June 10, 1970, at an emergency meeting in Amman, and was empowered to expel
members and deny them PLO resources.

what was considered one of their larger training camps. But if Israeli intelligence was correct about the location, size, and defenses of the position, it was faulty on the motivation of the fedayeen and their resolve to fight relentlessly.

The battle that ensued lasted for twelve hours, with the Palestinians, who had orders to stand fast, still in their bunkers and hitting back with a murderous hail of fire. After a while the Israelis discovered that they were far from getting the upper hand, and were in fact losing the battle and too many men. They retreated, fighting their way out with great difficulty and sustaining heavy casualties. Some of their tanks were left on the field of battle. The Israelis learned they were now fighting a different breed of men, and the Palestinians learned they were capable of standing up to regular army forces.

Similar encounters followed along the Israeli border in Jordan and particularly in southern Lebanon, where fierce fighting, raids, reprisals, shelling, counter-raids, and forays became the order of the day. On their part the Israelis suppressed news of any successes their enemies scored—for surely the Palestinians did not exist, and if they did it was only as semi-literate gangster refugees who had no business leaving their camps to indulge in guerrilla warfare. But if the Palestinian military escapades failed to leave a great impact on, or cause great disruption of, normal life in Israel, the border fighting claimed 80 percent of the more than 2,000 casualties sustained by Israel in the period from the 1967 war to the end of 1969.° Its economy also inevitably suffered from the labor shortages caused by the large number of men under arms, and the people's psychological makeup was undergoing a devastating change from living within the walls of fortress Israel, in a society continuously poised for military confrontations.

The guerrillas' greatest success, however, may have been the

° See Don Peretz, "Arab Palestine: Phoenix or Phantom?," *Foreign Affairs* (January 1970), p. 333. In a report that appeared in *Time*, December 13, 1968, it was said that Israel suffered 900 casualties from commando operations in 1968 alone. And according to the *New York Times* correspondent in Israel (May 18, 1968), there was "a gnawing suspicion among Israelis, denied vigorously and regularly by army spokesmen, that the casualty rate is even higher than officially admitted."

act of creating that new Palestinian consciousness toward which the young had been aching and groping for two decades. The movement attracted intellectuals, professionals, graduates, idealists, as well as alienated and deprived youngsters from the camps, of both sexes, people who had hitherto felt disenchanted with and disinherited by the Arabs and their world. In a short time the term Palestinian became identified not with the downtrodden refugee living in abject poverty, but with the young dedicated freedom fighter.

Soon the fedayeen were also enjoying wide support from the Arab masses and drawing subsidies from oil-rich countries in the area (particularly from Libya, where the civilian premier was a Palestinian from Haifa, and where there was a small community of refugees working as lawyers, doctors, teachers, and in other professions), and contributions from affluent Palestinians living in Kuwait and the Persian Gulf.

But because of their determined independence from the Arab governments, in whose lands they trained their men and from which they launched attacks across the border, the guerrillas found themselves at loggerheads with two of them: Jordan and Lebanon. In both of these countries they had, by threat of force, positioned themselves in strategic locations which came under their complete control. From time to time, the strikes they effected against Israel from these territories precipitated Israeli reprisal raids which disrupted the stability of life in Jordan and caused an exodus of villagers from southern Lebanon. At the same time, the governments of these states found it impossible to repress them or were loath to start a head-on confrontation with a movement that was immensely popular among the people of the Arab world.

However, as with every movement of its kind, the Palestinian resistance had to face hostile local forces that wished to see it crushed or restrained. In Jordan, the army was becoming alarmed at the increasing strength and autonomy of the fedayeen and angered by restrictions placed upon its officers by the king. They preferred to have the Palestinians moved, along with their stocks of arms, out of the towns, and to have them conduct their operations within the framework of Jordanian law and government bureaucracy. But a series of agreements signed by the authorities and the various guerrilla groups, designed to limit friction between the Bedouin army and the irrepressible Palestinians, failed to achieve a lasting settlement. Yasser Arafat and his fellow leaders were distrusted by the higher echelons in the military who suspected them of wanting to overthrow the monarchy, or, by virtue of the great power they enjoyed, establish a state within a state. The king's uncle, a man with a taste for sports cars and lavish summer villas who headed the Special Branch, was accused by the fedayeen of deliberately creating trouble in order to initiate a major clash and annihilate them.

The various agreements that were signed by King Hussein and Yasser Arafat, as head of the PLO, did not prevent bloody flare-ups from erupting from time to time. The Bedouins became more disenchanted with every concession the government made, and were bent on an all-out battle, the outcome of which, they felt certain, would be the total destruction of the guerrillas. In June 1970, when shooting broke out all over Jordan, pitting commandos against army forces and leaving 300 killed and wounded, the rift and enmity between the two groups widened. Three months later, on September 17, 1970, Jordan, now cut off from the rest of the world with the breakdown of transportation and communications systems, was engulfed in civil war.

The factors leading to this war may be found in the fact that the guerrillas' presence and life-style in Jordan, particularly in urban centers, was tantamount to a parallel government set up outside the law. They challenged, when they did not treat with contempt, the king and the army, and disrupted the business of the bourgeois classes. They earned a large measure of antagonism from the conservative sectors in the community by revolutionary pronouncements which gave rise to fears that some Palestinian leaders, notably George Habbash and Nayef Hawatmeh of the PDFLP, were bent on establishing "a godless communist republic." Guerrillas with Kalashnikov submachine guns were ubiquitous in Amman and other cities, acting independently of the law, organizing their own military police, road-check points, offices, newspapers, accreditations to foreign journalists, and military courts. They had intelligence agents in all levels of the government hierarchy and were thus informed beforehand of major decisions affecting their operation. They wanted, and there came a time when they did in actuality get, all the power in the land. Rephrasing the Bolshevik revolutionary cry of 1917, Nayef Hawatmeh was wont to say: "All power to the resistance." In Amman, guerrillas distributed handbills inviting officers of the Arab Legion "to join the ranks of the proletariat." Add to that the haughtiness and bravado displayed by individual commandos in their dealings with Jordanian bureaucrats and the large royal family and its hangers-on, who were at any rate, and particularly at that rate, hostile to them.

Behind all this lies yet another, more significant, factor responsible for impelling the fedayeen into their costly and fateful confrontation with the Royal Army. This was the large cultural gap that separated the Bedouin soldiers from the mostly urban and politically sophisticated Palestinians. The former were a nomadic people with traditions and a heritage derived exclusively from desert tribal society. There was little in their cultural and value structure that induced them to respond to the Palestinians' yearning for a homeland and a nation. The desert recognizes life as rotating around the head of the family, to whom loyalty is pledged unquestionably. Other tribes or communities, though populating an area within close proximity, are invariably looked upon as aliens and, except in the case of intermarriage, enemies. Indeed, tribal lore is replete with tales of "ghazzis," raids on one tribe by another in times of drought and famine. The defeated tribe would by custom live in disgrace until the day its men mounted a counter-raid, or "niquam" (revenge). Whether mounted as a "ghazzi" or "niquam," a tribal raid is usually of lightning speed and great savagery. There is no sustained fighting, no prolonged siege or planned military tactics. The fighters launch a surprise attack, kill, loot, and rape, and return with their booty across the desert to await the inevitable "niquam."

"Niquam" then, may have been what the Bedouin soldiers wanted. "Niquam" against those who subjected their tribe, the Arab Legion, and the head of their family, King Hussein, to repeated indignities. To those who study the details of the fighting in the Jordan civil war, patterns emerge that seem identical to a "ghazzi" or "niquam." The troops in most cases did not distinguish between fedayeen and ordinary citizens. Women and children were among the killed and wounded; houses were blown up; refugee camps were shelled and individual commandos on stretchers were savagely finished off. Some soldiers had smeared their faces black with soot to avoid being recognized by relatives of victims and thus become subject to vengeance in an individual "niquam."

As in a "niquam" raid, looting and rape were also rampant. In a report from Jordan by Eric Rouleau, published in *Le Monde Weekly*, December 16, 1970, we learn that "with the tacit agreement of their officers, the soldiers took to looting—a fact confirmed by many of the journalists who were witnesses. According to various reports, the Bedouins committed rape both in Amman and Zarqa; one of their victims was said to be the daughter of a high-ranking Jordanian diplomat."

Before the fighting broke out, it appears the king was under the impression that his troops could flush out the guerrillas within hours and destroy their operation once and for all, thereby fully re-establishing his authority, undermined and threatened by the commandos' growing strength and independence. When the Palestinians proved much more tenacious in their resistance, and as the fighting dragged on, then progressed into carnage, he was still determined to continue to the bloody end—particularly when his well-trained, well-supplied army of 60,000 men was getting the upper hand in the last days of the war.

Hussein had the steady backing of the United States government, which provided a continuous supply of arms and the possibility of intervention in the event of the tide turning against him. Nixon's visit to the Sixth Fleet and the veiled threats from the State Department were demonstrative proof of that.

The main battles of the civil war were waged in Amman and Zarqa, where systematic and sustained bombardments of refugee camps were carried out, with great loss of life not only to the guerrillas and their armed militia (who presumably mixed with the people, true to Maoist dictum, like fish in the water) but to civilians as well. In other parts of Jordan, little fighting took place and damage was comparatively minimal. In the north, the towns of Irbid, Jerash, and Salt were completely under fedayeen control and run as "soviets." Army troops encircled the towns and never at any stage attempted to march in, although they subjected guerrilla strongholds to heavy shelling from time to time.

By the end of the first week of fighting, the guerrillas were still holding out but were critically short of supplies and ammunition. No mass rebellion among the troops or defection of officers occurred. To avert that, the king had previously purged the army of men he thought of dubious loyalty and had prevented the infantry, which had a high proportion of Palestinians, from taking an active role in the fighting. Iraqi soldiers stationed in Jordan not only made no attempt to help the Palestinians, but folded their tents and pulled out of the area altogether. Syrian tanks that had moved into Jordan from the northern border were later recalled, presumably under pressure from President Nasser and the Russians, who had intelligence that the Americans were prepared to move into the country to aid Hussein in the event of "outside intervention." In his report on the civil war, Eric Rouleau wrote:

> It was obvious that the fedayeen could not hold out indefinitely. Deprived of valuable stocks of arms and munitions which were either seized or blown up, cut off from supply sources in Syria, short on food and water, they ran the risks—despite heroic resistance—of either slow starvation or sudden massacre.

The effect of the civil war on the Palestinian liberation movement was no less than devastating. Despite the agreements later signed by guerrilla representatives and the king that initially seemed to offer great concessions to the former and allow them continued independence, the prospects for the resistance were gloomy and its future in danger. The smaller groups were either absorbed by Al-Fatah or disappeared altogether. Their ranks were in disarray and needed time to reorganize. Most leaders of the resistance, particularly those of the PFLP and PDFLP, were harassed or hunted down by the authorities and had to lead semi-clandestine lives. Their offices were closed down and the groups' publication, *Al-Fatah*, was seized on a number of occasions. A coup in Syria had brought to power leaders not noted for their sympathy for the Palestinian revolution, and in Lebanon, Suleiman Franjiyeh, no lover of radical thought, was elected president of the republic.

The months following the hostilities were a time marked by a lull in activities—a search for alternatives, a calling into question of hitherto accepted assumptions, and a re-assessment of accomplishments and failures. A time of acute crisis when the major concern may have been: how can we insure our continued survival?

In Lebanon, the Palestinians had restricted their military operations to an area in the south that became known as Fatah-land, tactically connecting them with the guerrillas similarly positioned along the Israeli borders in Syria and Jordan. There they were less visible and not so vociferous. And although the large right-wing element in the country was responsible for a great deal of backlash, generating a lot of resentment against Palestinians in general and guerrillas in particular, the fedayeen enjoyed such wide support among the young and the educated that government attempts to restrict their operations were met by general strikes and protests.

As with the Special Branch in Amman, so it was in Beirut with the Deuxième Bureau, whose officials were mostly members of or closely allied to the Falangists. Like other indigenous people in former colonies who had admired their masters, the Falangists had acquired the superficial trappings, rather than the spirit, of the oppressor's culture. To them the Palestinians were anathema, and clashes, though not on a scale as bloody as those between the guerrillas and the army in Jordan, took place around the country. In April 1970, the Deuxième Bureau was exposed as having taken part in a plot to plunge the country into civil war by organizing bomb attacks against certain newspaper offices and religious establishments. The object was to foment a severe crisis that would be blamed on the Palestinians, and so bring the army into conflict with the various guerrilla groups. These specific charges were laid at the door of the Deuxième Bureau by no less a government official than Mr. Kamal Junblat, the then Minister of the Interior.°

Giving certain intelligence personnel twenty-four hours to quit, he also accused this organization of masterminding a plot on the lines of the scenario for Z, complete with the film's ingredients of a pro-American intelligence setup, a group of right-wing conspirators, muscle men, a rigged accident, and the unexpected presence of an enterprising photographer. The purpose of this was to cause civil war in Lebanon, Junblat claimed, a situation from which no one could benefit except those fanatic forces hostile to the fedayeen.

The first phase in this drama occurred on March 17 when three commando officers were called to an army check-point near Bint Jubail, in southern Lebanon, and shot dead on the spot. The army explained this as an "accident." As expected, pro-commando demonstrations were held in Beirut and other cities to protest the act; as planned, the Falangists held counter-demonstrations. This was sufficient to poison the air, and a severe gun battle took place a week later between guerrilla military police and "a gang of cigarette smugglers using commando uniforms" who were subsequently identified as Bureau agents or under Bureau protection. The result was four dead commandos and three dead "smugglers."

The next phase in this plot occurred the following day when a funeral cortege of a commando officer killed in the gun battle the previous evening passed through the town of Kahale. Well-directed machine-gun fire killed two people, and as the convoy went through the town on its way back that same day the commandos suffered seventeen killed in a second ambush. The gendarmes ordered to guard the convoy had mysteriously failed to appear, and official police reports had it that the Palestinians were firing into the air as they passed through the town; this, they speculated, may have started the shooting. However, a photographer who had accompanied the convoy on its return trip showed pictures of men in recognizably Falangist uniforms sighting their guns on the commandos.

° For a detailed account of this incident see the London *Economist*, April 11, 1970, p. 29.

This whole Deuxième Bureau operation failed, inasmuch as it did not attain its objective of stirring the Moslem and Christian communities in Lebanon to rise in a civil war and bring the army into the fray. It subsequently degenerated into a few days of gun battles between the Falangists and Palestinians around Sidon, Beirut, and Tyre.

In Syria, no opposition existed on the part of people or government to the activities conducted by the Palestinians or to the presence of their training camps around Damascus. In fact, the Syrians took a great pride in giving birth to Al-Saiqa, a relatively large group of 7,000, trained and supported by the Baathist regime, and allowed the fedayeen a free hand in opening recruiting offices and an independent radio station. In times of crisis, the Syrians were known to back the fedayeen in their ordeals with the Lebanese and Jordanian authorities. This support for the guerrillas was demonstrated adequately when Syrian tanks went to their aid during the Jordan civil war in September 1970.°

The notorious Dr. Habbash, however, was not a popular man with the Syrians, not so much because of his ideological extremism (a stance favored by the Damascus regime itself), but because of his exploits in terrorism and defiance of established Arab governments. Late in 1968, following the hijacking by his men of a plane belonging to a European airline and its landing in Damascus airport, he was taken into custody by the Syrians and placed in a security jail. This was later stormed by commandos from the PFLP with connections with prison authorities, who freed their leader and spirited him out of the country.

The presence of the guerrillas in other Arab states, notably Iraq,

---

° Anwar Sadat, the Egyptian president, declared that before his death Nasser had pressured the Syrians into exercising restraint by recalling these tanks, thus preventing outside powers from taking advantage of what was essentially an inter-Arab conflict. Yasser Arafat, in a press conference in Cairo on November 9, 1970 (from an AP dispatch in the *International Herald Tribune*, November 10, 1970), charged that American advisers took part in and directed the fighting against the fedayeen, and that the CIA instigated the war with the aim of destroying the guerrillas and liquidating the Palestinian revolution. Predictably, this charge was denied by the Pentagon and the State Department.

Algeria, Libya, and the United Arab Republic, remained restricted to training, fund raising, and liaison activities.

Despite the costs they paid in the Jordan civil war, despite King
Hussein's antagonism toward them, and despite the conspiracies
that continued to be directed against their operations by reactionary elements in the Middle East, the Palestinians were far
from crushed or inhibited in their activities. Indeed, their presence in the Arab world as a highly politicized group whose effect
was felt not only in terrorism and guerrilla warfare but also as a
revolutionary and progressive nucleus, became irreversible, just as
their emergence from the dust of the Six Day War had been inevitable.

In the relatively short time it took them to show the world
where they stood, the Palestinians demonstrated that theirs was a
liberation movement that would transcend the Arab rhetoric and
the Arab aims of yore. Freed of bitterness and despair, the New
Palestinians were learning who the real enemy was. They refused
to fall into the trap of racism and blind hate in which both Zionists
and Arabs were caught. A firm distinction was made between the
Jew and the Zionist, between returning to Palestine and annihi-
lating Israel, between liberation and persecution, between Abba
Eban and Isaac Deutscher, and a new image of the Jew was
formed. A dialogue with the New Israelis was conducted.°

Abu Iyad, one of the leaders of Al-Fatah, said in an interview
before his death at the hands of King Hussein's troops that the
Palestinian revolution condemned the persecution of human
beings by racists, and expressed the readiness of Al-Fatah to fight
alongside Jews anywhere in the world where they were being oppressed. The Palestinian revolutionist viewed his struggle as identical with the one waged by all the wretched of the earth for liberation and dignity.† The Palestinian guerrillas thus trained Black

---

° At the Congress of the Palestinian Revolution, held in Amman in July 1970,
many of the guests who arrived to demonstrate their solidarity with the Palestinian
liberation movement were European and American Jews as well as Israelis.

† See *Al-Taleea* for June 1969 in *Basic Political Documents of the Palestinian
Resistance* (Beirut: Palestine Research Center, 1970). Abu Iyad fell in battle

Panthers, members of the Front for the Liberation of Quebec, Eritreans, Yemenis, Gulf Arabs, Kurds, and other freedom fighters who came to their camps for training. Some of these, as in the case of the latter groups, were engaged in wars *against* the Arabs.

In Beirut on August 12, 1970, when the Deuxième Bureau planted bombs outside the temples in the Jewish quarter to terrorize the people, an Al-Fatah detachment went to the area and stood guard in the streets to prevent whatever nefarious crimes the Falangist thugs intended to perpetrate. Other events and pronouncements over the years were too spontaneous to have been craftily manipulated for the purposes of propaganda and public relations.

In a report on Colonel Qadafi in the London *Observer* (January 24, 1971), John Bonar explained how Colonel Qadafi's expropriation of Jewish property in Libya antagonized the Palestinians. "When Yasser Arafat visited Libya in November, he thanked the Libyan people for their support, not the government. The reason was obvious; while the Palestinians were busy telling everyone that they were fighting Zionists, not Jews, Colonel Qadafi was expropriating Jewish property and expelling Jews from Libya."

The Palestinians' political stance vis-à-vis the Israelis, the Arabs, and the world was seen in their vocal claims that the conflict between Arabs and Israelis stemmed exclusively from their own plight and dealt with issues that had to do with their own destiny and their place in history. The search for peace in the area hinged on the fate of the West Bank refugees, and of Palestinian property and territory held by Israel—all directly Palestinian concerns—but they were conceded no right to a voice in these negotiations. The search for a settlement was being pursued with the UAR, Syria, and Jordan—governments that were far removed from having a direct stake, a direct interest, or a direct right to involvement in these issues. The Palestinians knew that the Arab governments and their big power patrons would not hesitate to

---

against Jordanian troops in the mountains of Ajlun in July 1971. He was generally considered one of the top men in the movement. At the time of his death he was thirty-four years old.

sacrifice their fundamental aspirations at the conference table, and thus they were determined not to allow a sellout of their cause, or a peace initiative that did not reflect their entity as a nation party to the dispute.

The cease fire that the Americans succeeded in arranging among the Israelis, the Egyptians, and the Jordanians in August 1970, to be followed by peace talks, was rejected by the guerrillas for those same reasons. Point Four in the Seven Points passed by the Central Committee of Al-Fatah, January 1969, had stated:

> Al-Fatah, the Palestine national liberation movement, categorically rejects the Security Council Resolution of November 22, 1967, and the Jarring Mission to which it gave rise. This resolution ignores the national rights of the Palestinian people—failing to mention its existence. Any solution claiming to be peaceful which ignores this basic factor will thereby be doomed to failure. In any event, the acceptance of the resolution of November 22, 1967, or any pseudo-political solution, by whatsoever party, is in no way binding upon the Palestinian people, who are determined to pursue mercilessly their struggle against foreign occupation and Zionist colonization.

Eight months later, Yasser Arafat reiterated, in an interview published in *Free Palestine*: "Let no one think that any resolution taken outside the will of the Palestinians will ever acquire viability or legality."

If the Palestinians alone were not strong enough to defeat Israel, they alone were strong enough to defeat efforts for a settlement reached over their heads. This was demonstrated when the Rogers peace plan was temporarily paralyzed by the guerrillas' intensification of shelling and attacks against the Israeli borders and a spectacular display of hijacking and blowing up of civilian aircraft on the territory of the same Arab governments that had initially accepted the cease fire. The fireworks and drama at Cairo airport and Dawson airfield were a contemptuous reminder to the Arabs that their two-decade-long game of pawn politics was intolerable and past its time. The contempt shown the Western governments in the destruction of their coveted symbols of technology and opulence was a slap in the face to those who, thousands of miles away, would sit in their seats of power to decide the fate of weaker nations and people.

In the months that followed the Jordan civil war it became obvious that if the Middle East, and the world, were to get peace, the Palestinians were the only group which could ultimately make it, or make it possible; for if the Arabs could not control the guerrillas then they could not truly offer proposals for a settlement unacceptable to the PLO. After the June War, whenever resolutions were passed, meetings were held, or efforts were made in the direction of a settlement, the Palestinians reacted by asserting their presence, their viewpoint, and their power to reveal that what the Arab governments were after and what they themselves were after were two different things. The Egyptians may have wanted to "liquidate the traces of Israeli aggression" and liberate their piece of Sinai Desert, the Syrians to reclaim their mountain ridge on the Golan Heights, and the Jordanian government (except for the Palestinians, who were three-quarters of the population) to recognize the Israeli status quo in return for the West Bank. But the Palestinians were struggling for their homeland, and Palestinian leaders, whether extremists, moderates, irredentists, revolutionaries, ideologues, or theoreticians recognized this and became ever more unified in their joint battle with almost everyone else that mattered.

All through the winter months of 1971 the Palestinians followed the pages of a different calendar from that of the Arabs and the Israelis, the Russians and the Americans. The Israelis and the Arabs issued their respective set of conditions for peace, while the two big powers, anxious to oversee or impose a settlement, waited in the background to untangle that skein of many threads that is the Middle East conflict. The Palestinians, on the other hand, still recovering from the ravages of the Jordan war, which had left thousands of guerrillas and militia killed and had depleted their stocks of arms, were regrouping and restructuring their ranks. There were unsettled questions about their future and, with almost daily shoot-outs between fedayeen and Bedouins, uncertainty about their modus operandi. There was talk of going underground, of

creating a Palestinian government in exile, of forming one liberation front, of fragmenting into cadres.

At this stage the resistance, with bases still intact in southern
Lebanon and Syria, continued to be militarily and politically viable. One danger confronting it, however, was potential loss of its
safe rear—that is, of mass support and the opportunity to continue
organizing and recruiting in the cities and the camps, particularly
in Jordan where the bulk of the Palestinians lived.° A deadlier
hazard was the concerted and intensified efforts, coming close on
the heels of the September fighting, to crush the revolution
mounted by Western neo-imperialism, on the one hand, and the
pro-imperialist oligarchies, bourgeois alliances, and feudal classes
that dominated Middle Eastern politics on the other.

So long as the Palestinian resistance had been of use to the Arab
regimes, it was supported; but such support only came while the
guerrillas were seen to advance Arab aims of return of occupied
territory through fedayeen pressure on Israel. Now that moves
were being made to implement the November 1967 UN resolution
and follow the so-called Rogers peace plan, the complete destruction of the resistance became a precondition for "an honorable solution." This view was subscribed to not only by Hussein, but by
Egypt and other Arab regimes who merely left it to the King to
see this realized at a time and place of his choosing.†

Less than a year after thousands of men, women, and children

° In 1967, the Palestinian population numbered around 2.4 million of whom 57
percent were refugees and 43 percent non-refugees. The latter category refers to
Palestinians who on the eve of the 1948 war had lived, and continued to live, in the
West Bank (20 percent), Gaza (6 percent), Israel (12 percent), and other places (5
percent). In 1967, the Palestinian population was dispersed in the following places:
Jordan (52 percent), Gaza (17 percent), Israel (12 percent), Lebanon (7 percent),
Syria (6 percent), and other places—North Africa, Persian Gulf, Canada, Australia,
USA—(6 percent). (In *Mallaf el-Kadiyya el-Falasteenia* [Beirut: Palestine Research
Center, 1968], pp. 65–66.)

† It should be noted that during the Jordanian civil war, when it was assumed
that the fedayeen would be crushed overnight, the Egyptian government remained
silent for the first three days and it was not till Arab workers, students, peasants,
and members of left-wing groups and parties took to the streets in the Arab capitals that Nasser proceeded to voice his protests.

fell in the civil war in Jordan, Hussein and his Bedouins moved again. This was a mere winding-up of a job that had been begun ten months before by the Jordanians in collusion with Egypt and some governments in the Levant. The time, place, and situation chosen were most suitable for the triumph of Arab reaction: when the Jordanian army went on the offensive against the Palestinians, it did so at a time when attention in the Arab world was diverted to events in Morocco and Sudan, where two abortive coups had just taken place; the fedayeen were at the time holed up in the Ajlun and Jerash hills in the open or in caves, with little ammunition, supplies, food, or water; and Hussein was fully aware of the positive response that his move would elicit from the Arab leaders.

He knew, for example, that none of these leaders had shown any desire to intervene, even protest, during the many months his troops were placing mines along the banks of the Jordan River at points where commandos crossed into occupied and Israeli territory; when they ambushed individual fedayeen and shot them dead; and when they instigated minor skirmishes in the hills northwest of Amman to create an atmosphere of tension preceding an all-out attack.

In the middle of July the Royal Army, supported by tanks, artillery, and fighter planes, attacked guerrilla positions and subjected them to continuous bombardment. With only thirty-one of its men dead, according to a Jordanian spokesman, the army finally won a battle that raged for ten days and in which the Bedouins' savagery in war was again demonstrated in all its chilling cruelty. Those first few fedayeen who surrendered were butchered on the spot; the injured were shown no mercy and were finished off. Among the prisoners who were later taken into custody mass executions were carried out, and the "bad guerrillas" who wanted to create "a godless republic" were separated from the "good guerrillas" who did not. Some of those who opted not to surrender and wandered the mountains without food or water, were chased by the army and finished off or captured. Scores escaped into the West Bank and gave themselves up to the Israelis rather than face torture at the hands of the Bedouins. The fedayeen military base in Jordan was now wiped out. Offensives to liquidate their political base in Lebanon and Syria were mounted.

The ebb and flow that are the natural condition of every revolutionary struggle were confronting the Palestinian movement. A shift to a different front and to different directions became essential. One manifestation of this became evident in the reversal of the stand that the PFLP and Al-Fatah had each adopted apropos of the revolutionary situation. Whereas the former had contended the triumph of the Palestinian revolution would be achieved by becoming integrated within the *whole* Arab revolution (whose aim was to defeat imperialism as well as Zionism in the Arab world through protracted war on a broad front), the latter in contrast believed that the one should precede the other. Now the Palestinians of Al-Fatah came to realize that the revolution's *raison d'être* did in actuality lie in a wider confrontation with imperialism and foreign domination in the Arab world and, more than that, that Al-Fatah's official position of neutrality vis-à-vis domestic politics in its host countries had been unwise.° And the PFLP for its part was reminded of the military limitations of the resistance as a direct instrument for eradicating the reactionary status quo and its accompanying class structure in the various regions of the Arab world.

In the Gaza Strip, guerrilla war and resistance to Israeli occupation appeared to be responding independently of events in Jordan and the Arab world. Indeed, they seemed to intensify with every reversal the fedayeen suffered in Jordan and elsewhere. The Gazans—half of whose number in the camps average twenty-three years of age—are a more rugged breed than those living under occupation in the West Bank and have much less to lose. In the past,

---

° There were many Palestinians (including this writer), as well as other members of the revolutionary left in the Arab world, who felt mortified to see a front-page picture of Yasser Arafat shaking hands with King Hussein—and smiling broadly— soon after the September massacres and the so-called Cairo Accords. The picture was presumably to symbolize the end of hostilities and "return to cooperation and non-interference" between the Palestinians and the Jordanian government.

long before the June War, the Gazans had also been trained in weapons and fighting, for despite their revulsion toward the Egyptian military officers who had administered the territory from 1948 until the advent of the Israelis, the Palestinians of Gaza were indebted to the Egyptians for a thorough education in the use of arms. Whereas before the outbreak of the Six Day War the Palestinians in Jordan had been ruthlessly hindered by King Hussein from forming a base of any kind in the country, the Gazans had already established at least one sound military one. And whereas resistance had subsided on the West Bank, the commandos in Gaza —whose allegiance was to the PFLP rather than Al-Fatah, which had virtually suspended operations there since 1970—stepped up their attacks against Israeli patrols and against collaborators, and sporadically obstructed 6,000 or so Gazans from going in buses to work daily in Israel.°

In January 1971, Israel made an effort to combat this by establishing a concentration camp in Abu Enaima, an abandoned manganese port sixty miles south of the Suez Canal on the Gulf of Suez and *about 150 miles from Gaza itself,* where they held 129 men, women, and children in detention. In the Israeli Knesset, on March 8, 1971, General Dayan admitted that these twenty-nine families of "suspected Gaza Strip terrorists" had been held there for more than nine weeks after a major offensive against the guerrillas, but denied a communist deputy's charge that their detention was under concentration camp conditions. He added that this was part of a deliberate policy by the Israeli authorities to deny guerrillas "aid, shelter, and comfort" afforded by their families.†

But Israeli repression in Gaza was consistently matched by intensified resistance. The occupiers' policy of demolishing houses that belonged to the families of guerrillas or suspected guerrillas, a policy that seemed to work in their favor on the West Bank, met stiff opposition in Gaza. Going one step further than they had done on the West Bank, the Israelis decided to break up the larger

---

° Justification for this was found in the contention that for every Palestinian working in Israel, an Israeli is relieved for duties in the army.

† Report in *International Herald Tribune,* March 9, 1971, p. 2.

camps in Gaza, move the families that had lived in them into isolated regions of the Strip, and impose stricter and more brutal controls on the movement of peasants, workers, shopkeepers, students, and other inhabitants of the region.

On the day in July 1971 when the Israeli forces moved their bulldozers to demolish houses that the refugees had lived in for over twenty years, the people and the resistance reacted with violence. "The occupants of the houses had been warned beforehand," we are told in a special report in the London *Observer* from Gaza. "But many refused to leave their homes. In order to avoid burying them alive, the Israeli soldiers went into the houses and drove them out—the women and children proved especially obdurate—with blows from sticks and batons. Within a few days . . . fifty houses had crumbled into dust and 500 people, half of them young children, were homeless." °

A spontaneous reaction to this from the fedayeen as well as the people was not long in coming. "That night," the *Observer* report continues, "there was more violence than usual in Gaza. A ferocious, suicidal gun and grenade battle between the Israelis and five young Fatah guerrillas broke out just after dawn in one of the UNRWA schools. Two hours later, all the fedayeen were dead, one of them leaving his silhouette in blood, hair, and entrails on the schoolroom walls. The following day, as small girls collected flowers for the dead, a swirling mob of hysterical women from Jabalia Camp besieged the UNRWA headquarters. There have been several more angry demonstrations in the past week as the total of demolished houses has soared to 400."

The inference, the *Observer* report concludes, is that neither a benevolent occupation in Gaza nor pursuit of "the stick policy" as characterized by "the heavy-handed repression of January and February" that preceded the methodical destruction to rubble of refugee homes has worked.† "Nor has the steady pulse of vio-

---

° August 4, 1971, p. 4. Special report from John de St. Jorre in Gaza.

† In January, the biggest camp in Gaza was *sealed off for a whole month* to enable the occupying authorities to conduct a house-to-house search for arms. Gunbutt-happy border troops, supported by the baton-happy police, filled up hospital wards in "eight weeks of terror."

lence, both against the Israeli soldiers and Arab collaborators, diminished. Gaza is the only place where the Palestinian resistance
("terrorism" to the Israelis) at a terrible cost and with suicidal te-
nacity, is worthy of the name."

Following its military reversals in Jordan and the shift in the political priorities of the revolution, the Palestinians again regrouped
and reconsidered their emphasis and their aims. Although it was
obvious the Palestinians would never lay down their arms and accept a return to that state of quiescence that existed before 1967,
the overwhelming impression in the Arab world following the second defeat in Jordan, fostered by irresponsible press reports and
idle speculation, was that the Palestinians' military and political
effectiveness were virtually over. Through all this, the Arabs and
the Israelis, the Russians and the Americans resumed their maneu-
verings to achieve a settlement in the Middle East. The link that
bound Zionism and Arab reactionary regimes and their petty-
bourgeois classes was strengthened, and the Palestinians reorgan-
ized for the next phase in their armed struggle.

5. What Is to Be Done?

The tragedy of the Arabs and the Israelis in the Middle East has been that they suffered the consequences of not limiting or identifying their objectives. The Arabs, whose objective should have been (in the absence of a spontaneous desire to accept the diktat) the containment of Israel rather than its confrontation, adopted policies that were sure to activate a groundswell for war, war from which only the Israelis could emerge as victors. For twenty years the field of expression of the will of the Arab people was left in the hands of demagogues and fanatics, and their energies were channeled into challenging the physical existence of the state of Israel and the Jews living in it.

At a time when the memory of the gas chambers was still imprinted on the minds of the peoples of the world, and in particular the Western world, this policy helped, obversely, the Israeli cause rather than that of the Arabs. No better example could serve to illustrate this than those weeks that preceded the Six Day War, when blood-curdling threats could be heard all around the Arab world threatening Israel with destruction and its people with a sea of blood. While the Arabs were making their irresponsible statements and appearing as aggressors in world public opinion, the Israelis were preparing for war and expansion and seen as the victims.

Despite the absurdity of the Zionist claim for a "return" to Palestine and the injustice inherent in the act of taking from the Palestinians to give to the Jews for a crime committed by the Nazis, the real issues involved in the Palestinian problem and the hopes for its solution got buried under the heavy weight of the first speech pledging the driving of the Jews into the sea. Had the Arabs had the wisdom to devise an effective stance vis-à-vis Israel, their efforts might have gone instead into restricting the predictable expansionism of the "Jewish state" and adopting a sober program to inform the world of the nature of their grievance. So without an adequate approach to dealing with the Zionists and a true understanding of their own limitations, the Arabs were destined to relive their failures in a vacuum. The promises and speeches that thoughtless Arab leaders gave to the masses, like pills, to make the Israeli pain go away, were a manifestation of this inability to realistically broach "the Palestine problem." And although year in, year out, the Israelis were still very much around, and proving it on the battlefield, no re-evaluation of that position occurred.

The fuzzy hopes the Arabs had of dislodging Israel vanished upon waking up on June 5, 1967, a few shattering moments after Israeli Phantoms eluded Egyptian radar and destroyed the entire air force of the United Arab Republic. This was indeed a moment as shattering as the 1948 Israeli victory over the combined forces of the Arab armies. In both events the Israelis presented the Arabs with a *fait accompli* and a set of "non-negotiable" claims on seized property and annexed land. But whereas the first military defeat was followed by confusion and upheaval, the second precipitated the only diplomatic offensive the Arab world ever mounted in their dispute with the Zionists.

Israeli failure to acknowledge the implications of their presence in the midst of the Arab world, and the geopolitical demands that that presence made, resulted in continued frustration of their efforts to be recognized and accepted. For they wanted to create a "Jewish State" oriented to European culture and allied to the West—in that part of the Third World that is fiercely suspicious of the Occident and its imperialistic machinations and hostile to the memory of its inglorious past. Instead of adopting the objective of becoming an integral part of the Middle East, it persisted in clinging to the concept of a "European rampart."

The Arabs of the Levant, not comprehending the designs of a state "as Jewish as England is English," viewed the Israelis as the Algerians had viewed the *pieds noirs*. The *colons* had taken their French culture to the Maghreb and continued to identify themselves as Frenchmen; in like manner the Jewish immigrants in Palestine, and later in the rigidly sectarian state of Israel, were seen as encapsulating themselves within a European culture alien to the Middle East. Although the parallel was inconsistent, that at least was how the arrogant and militarily superior Israelis were seen by the Arabs in whose midst they lived. Thus the Israelis also created for themselves a vacuum into which they fell, their hopes as irreconcilable as those of their Arab counterparts, their reality and their dialectics precluding an effective achievement of Zionist aims.

One may ask, at this juncture, and under these circumstances, what in fact was the result of the Zionist experiment?

From the outset, it revealed the weaknesses inherent in an exclusively "sectarian," "tribal," "Moslem," "Christian," or "Jewish" state. One does not have to ransack the annals of history for proof of the destructive propensities these states acquire and how far removed they become from the faith they set out to reflect. As for Israel, the murderous zeal that went into the creation of it surely could not have so much stemmed from the ethics and noble teachings of Judaism as from the naive, nationalistic sophistry and simplistic tenets of *Der Judenstaat*. For the whole humanistic tradition of Jewishness would be shaken if identified with the massacres of Deir Yassin and Kafr Qassem in the past, and the spectacle of an occupying power in the present. It is evident that the state of Israel has not distinguished itself in the twenty-three years since its creation as an expression of the true spirit, the true dignity, and the true creativity of Jewishness. Moreover, it has failed even in the mission that its original Zionist pioneers designed for it.

"After more than fifty years of Zionist activities—among them many decades over the international diplomatic front—and on looking back on the experiences gained in the twenty years of existence of the state of Israel," writes the noted Zionist leader, Nahum Goldmann, "I am beginning to have doubts as to whether the establishment of the state of Israel as it is today . . . was the fullest accomplishment of the Zionist idea and its twofold aim: to save the Jews from discrimination and persecution by giving them the opportunity for a decent and meaningful life . . . second, to ensure the survival of the Jewish people against the threat of disintegration and disappearance in those parts of the world where they enjoy full equality of rights." °

The state of Israel, whether viewed as a colonial phenomenon or the rightful homeland of the Jewish people (and how many homelands, as I.F. Stone has asked, might have to be reshuffled if claims as old as the Jews have in Palestine were to be redeemed?), has hardly succeeded in its aim of making a home for the "ingathering of the exiles" or the loftier aim of being the center for the rejuvenation and enhancement of the Jewish consciousness. For those many emancipated Jews, living comfortably and free of hindrance around the world, Israel offers a less attractive alternative in a lifestyle geared for military confrontation, in a society perpetually threatened and perpetually threatening, a society that is a de-

---

° "The Future of Israel," *Foreign Affairs* (April 1970), p. 443.

cidedly false measure of the Jewish traditions that had imprinted themselves on countless civilizations, cultures, and nations.

Nor has Israel been instrumental in bringing about or hastening the liquidation of anti-Semitism. Its creation has indeed helped that to emerge in places where anti-Zionism, as in the Middle East, was reflected in persecution of local Jewry. Tiny Israel, the miracle in the desert, Eretz Israel, has been impossibly at odds not only with the Arabs, but with itself, with the age, and with history. Shooting its way to peace and a place in the community of men has not been to any avail.

The uniqueness of the conflict in the Middle East, as three wars have shown, makes the myth and euphoria of Israeli military triumphs appear for what they are: mythical and euphoric, for these will not hide the fact that in twenty-three years of military confrontations between Arabs and Israelis there really has been neither victor nor vanquished, that the failure of one has been the failure of both, and that if one paid a price for defeat the other paid a price for victory. Where the Arabs, in the aftermath of each war, were left more disunited, stunned, mortified, and closer to bankruptcy than before, reduced to agitating for a mere return to the status quo ante, their enemy neither destroyed nor closer to being driven into the sea, the Israelis were trading one insecure border for another, allocating larger amounts of their budget for armaments, enlisting more men in their military forces who would otherwise have been of better use in the labor force, and continuing to live with more tension looming ahead, poised nervously for the next inevitable confrontation. If "Asian barbarism" was learning little from the tempo and reality of the times, the "European rampart" was learning less from the follies of arrogance.

However, developments that followed the Six Day War indicated that we were witnessing the first major effort in the history of the Arab-Israeli conflict to establish conditions under which the peoples of the Middle East can live in tolerable stability. This effort also revealed a dramatic change in the thinking and policy planning of the Arabs, and particularly the Egyptians. The Arabs of the Levant came to recognize the durability of the Israeli presence and no longer sought its destruction, although no trend toward rapproachment with the Zionists has gained much strength. The Egyptians, on the other hand, appeared to be heading toward formal recognition of the Zionist state, an end of all hostilities, and the signing of a peace treaty. In making the latter conditional on Israeli withdrawal from the Sinai—that is to say, occupied Egyptian territory rather than occupied Arab territory—they were opting for a separate settlement and leaving the Levantines to make their own deal.

The United Arab Republic was thus serving notice on the Arabs that it was suspending its leadership of their world and returning to the position that prevailed before the first war when Egypt was essentially a north African nation whose people identified themselves as Egyptians, with vague ties to the Levant based on language, religion, and culture. This policy was nothing less than a reversal of the grandiose schemes that the late President Nasser had devised to lead, mobilize, and unite the Arab world.

The Israelis, confronted by this phenomenon and suspicious of Egyptian intentions, were slow in taking advantage of the initiative to secure that peace they had constantly proclaimed to be their only aim. Hence neither the government nor any politically influential group worked in favor of a genuine compromise. Even when negotiations through Gunnar Jarring, the United Nations representative, were going on, the Israelis were proceeding with building projects on seized Arab land in occupied Jerusalem, continuing to develop sizable communities in Sharm el-Sheikh and planning to annex, along with the Holy City, a broad strip of territory along the Jordan River ("for paramilitary settlements") and the Golan Heights.

Although in the past the Israelis had contended that the only stumbling block to peace was the Arabs' refusal to recognize Israel as a sovereign state, in the face of Egyptian willingness to sign a treaty they held that peace was contingent on Arab acceptance of "secure, agreed, and recognized borders," which meant major changes in the map in favor of an Israeli interpretation of "security." As negotiations gathered momentum, the Zionists consolidated their grip on the West Bank and accelerated their efforts to build 19,500 high-rise apartments in Jerusalem and intensive settlements in Hebron. In Jerusalem more than 4,000 acres of Arab land were expropriated for a building project which was to accommodate exclusively Jewish families. Israeli Housing Minister Ze'ev Sharef declared that Israel was determined that Jerusalem remain "an emphatically Jewish city. This is a plan with a Jewish goal. This is a Zionist exhibition." ° This was pointed to by the Arabs as proof that Israel was not sincere about peace or about giving up occupied land.

In peace negotiations, the Israeli concern was to deal directly with Egypt and thereby isolate it from the eastern front states, rendering the Syrian, Lebanese, and Jordanian positions more helpless. Syria, a country that had had nine military coups and six different constitutions in twenty-three years, remained erratic in its stance and rejected outright both the November 1967 UN Resolution and any contact with Jarring. Lebanon, which had lost no territory to the enemy and had not been engaged in any serious fighting, was passive. Jordan continued to be reluctant about spelling out explicitly in public its definition of an acceptable settlement, although it was reported to have conducted secret face-to-face negotiations with the Zionists.

This left the Palestinians, the group in the region with the highest stake, in a dilemma at a time when they were expected to maintain their political dynamism. They had just emerged from the Jordan civil war, which had left them weaker as a military entity, and were now contending with sustained pressure from King Hussein, the loss of Syrian support, and the defection of Egypt. There was talk of setting up a Palestinian state and bargaining over occupied territory which, except for Sinai and the Golan Heights, was Palestinian territory.

What were they, faced with overwhelming obstacles, to do to achieve their long-standing aims of a democratic, unitary, and secular state in Palestine? Were they to proclaim continued and un-

---

° *Time*, March 1, 1971, p. 15.

compromising attachment to total liberation of their homeland or acquiesce in a settlement that involved the establishment of a Palestine state? Were the options open to them limited to these two alternatives?

Wildly simplistic statements about what to do with us continued to be made up till the time of the battle of Karameh, on March 21, 1968. Before that most proposals advanced by interested parties dealt flatly with "absorption of Arab refugees." As recently as 1967, when the June War gave rise to speculation on the fate of "Arab refugees," Mr. Walter Laqueur, a well-known expert on the Middle East and the director of the Institute of Contemporary History in London, voiced the sentiments of many of those who bothered to write or read about us when he said: "The refugee problem *could* be solved—an international loan of several billion dollars would make their absorption possible, some on the west bank, others in underpopulated regions of Iraq and Syria." * One wonders what made this gentleman so confident that the Palestinians were ready to accept that when for over two decades they had adamantly refused monetary compensation, absorption, and "billion dollar loans"; and what it was about the underpopulated regions of Iraq and Syria that would have seemed so attractive to the Palestinians then that did not before.

Even better informed commentators fumbled in accentuating the question of compensation and resettlement. Professor Arnold Toynbee, long an advocate of the rights of the refugees and "a Western spokesman for the Arab cause," betrayed this in an exchange of letters about the possibility of peace in the Middle East between himself and J.L. Talmon, professor of modern history at the Hebrew University of Jerusalem.† Dr. Toynbee proposed that the first step toward peace would be a simultaneous declaration by the Arab states and the Palestinians pledging themselves to

---

* "Is Peace in the Middle East Possible," in *The Israel-Arab Reader: A Documentary History of the Middle East Conflict,* Walter Laqueur, ed. (New York: Citadel Press, 1969).

† The letters, dated July 1967, appeared in *Encounter* (October 1967), pp. 68–77.

recognize Israel and make peace with it on "approximately the 1948 armistice line." Israel in turn would make a similar pledge accepting these frontiers with the intention of making peace and undertaking to bring about "a satisfactory permanent settlement of the problem of the 1948 refugees." These reciprocal pledges, Dr. Toynbee suggested, would open the way for a negotiated treaty and then "things that have so far been impossible would become possible." He enumerated four points that might lead to peace. Of these, three dealt with the "conversion of the 1948 armistice lines into permanent frontiers," water for irrigation and desalination, a right of way through the Suez and the Straits of Tiran, and other perennial irritants characterizing the Arab-Israeli conflict. The fourth point purported to solve the refugee problem by offering the Palestinians monetary compensation for the loss of their property situated in Israel and an extra indemnity for having been forced to suffer for twenty years as innocent victims. The refugees, he added, should be given the option of either returning to their homes as "loyal citizens of Israel" or settling elsewhere. Those who did not accept the condition of becoming bona fide Israeli citizens would find help in a fund that would be raised for their resettlement outside the Jewish state. "I am sure the majority will opt for resettlement outside Israel," he stated.

Dr. Toynbee was, of course, speaking of the fate and welfare of individuals rather than the destiny of a nation. He was right in asserting that most refugees would not return to Israel on the condition that they live as "loyal Israeli citizens." In toto, his solution, not unlike others before it, denied the Palestinians the opportunity for a decent existence in their own homeland and guaranteed their ultimate disappearance as an entity and a people—a fate they had tenaciously fought against. At any rate, one would hardly have given the Israeli authorities high marks as benevolent caretakers of minority groups in their exclusive state in order to entice a refugee to return to his homeland as "a loyal Israeli citizen."

It is interesting to note the inevitable response to Dr. Toynbee's suggestions from the Israeli side. Professor Talmon wrote that "all but one" of his correspondent's four points would be readily met. He was agreeable to "monetary compensation, extra-indemnity, participation in an international fund for resettlement. The difficulty would frankly be the suggestion of an Israeli offer to the Arab refugees of 1948 of the choice of returning home." For if this were allowed, Professor Talmon claimed, "it would impose upon the refugees . . . strains and stresses which they would be spared if resettled in an Arab land or overseas." His own solution was for a separate accord with Jordan whose king, after initially weathering the storm for having come to terms with Israel, would find that the Arab states would tire of the excitement and gradually slide into a modus vivendi with Israel or follow Hussein's example. It was not revealed if he had any fears whether Hussein himself would follow Abdulla's example.

"I believe, like you," he said, "that the international community, especially the West, would be enthusiastically ready to offer very large sums and sponsor a joint international venture, with Israel and Jordan as partners, designed to resettle the refugees and execute those public works of irrigation and desalination you mention, solving thereby not only the refugee problem, but restoring Hussein to his former position. A common stake in joint prosperity would thus be created. Would Hussein dare take such a step alone?"

At any rate, Hussein did not. He opted instead, only three years later, to burn his capital and unleash his Bedouins on three-quarters of his population.

With the emergence of the New Palestinians, debate over resettlement and large loans ceased. In other words, only when we took to armed violence did the world stop calling us "the Arab refugees" and start calling us Palestinians. Responsible statements were heard from world leaders suggesting that for the first time since their diaspora, the Palestinian people's position was now being understood. President Nixon, a man not noted for his consideration of the oppressed peoples of the world, said in his State of the World message in February 1971 that no Middle East peace was possible "without addressing the legitimate aspirations of the Palestinian people." This was significant only inasmuch as it indicated the great shift toward understanding the Palestinian cause, occurring in American policy, and in that it was the first statement of its kind made by an American president.

The only sympathetic response to, or at least understanding of, the Palestinians from the Israeli side, came from the New Israelis. The Old Israelis remained adamant that either the Palestinians did not exist or that they would one day conclude a separate peace with Hussein. They were the archetypal Zionists, aging Eastern Europeans who believed blindly in Zionist claims in Palestine and contemptuously dismissed competing ones. To them the Palestinians were the "natives" who, unbeknownst to the Zionists, had been illegally inhabiting the Jewish Promised Land. Driven out, the Palestinians would soon vanish into thin air. Their existence was not recognized in the same manner that Israel's existence was not recognized by the Arabs.

The New Israelis were the young men and women in Israel who did not feel the insecurity and frustration of older Zionists, who were prepared to acknowledge the validity of the Palestinian entity, and who were not blind to Palestinian national aspirations. Shlomo Avineri, a representative of this group and chairman of the Department of Political Science at the Hebrew University in Jerusalem, declared bluntly that the Palestinians were the only people in the Middle East who could offer peace to Israel and with whom Israel should deal directly. He condemned the hard and unrealistic position that those on the other side of the generational gap adopted. "A typical example of the older generation," he said, "is the Prime Minister, Golda Meir. Despite her tough-mindedness, Mrs. Meir would be an accommodating and reasonable negotiator with any of the Arab states; when it comes to the Palestinian Arabs, however, she is hard as rock." °

Two other spokesmen of the New Israelis were Chaim Herzog and Elad Peled, both of whom were engaged in intelligence work and thus had first-hand contact with and knowledge of Palestinians. The former saw the issue pragmatically. "I believe," he said, "that we have no chance of achieving any settlement with the Arab world except through the Palestinians." The latter, who preferred the moral approach, said: "During the years of the conflict, the Palestinian Arab community asserted its national self-identity.

° "The Palestinians and Israel," *Commentary* (June 1970), p. 41.

. . . In the same way that we have claimed national self-determination for ourselves, we have to recognize it also for those who live alongside us." °

The growing awareness of Palestinian aspirations among perceptive Israelis did not extend to sympathy for the Al-Fatah concept of a secular Palestine and the return of the Palestinians to their homeland. But the departure from the hard Zionist line was in itself revealing. Avineri, in his *Commentary* article, cites his objection to a binational state. "Over the last century the Jews and the Palestinian Arabs have merged into national movements, each craving a home, a place in the sun, a corner of the earth it can call its own. Throwing both of them into a state which would be neither Jewish nor Arab would make it impossible for either movement to overcome mutual tension and start cooperating with the other." But he adds: "On the other hand, those like Golda Meir, who continue to ask 'Who are the Palestinians?' seem increasingly out of touch with reality; for it is Palestinian organizations that send their members to kill and maim Israelis, and it is against members of Palestinian organizations that Israeli patrols lie in nightly ambush in the Jordan Valley. Under such conditions anyone still questioning the existence of Arabs who call themselves Palestinian is talking ideology not facts."

The Palestinians currently find themselves confronted by the choice of taking either one of two roads. They can consider a solution *now* that departs, in one degree or another, from their set aims of a secular state in Palestine; or they can continue the struggle until the whole of their homeland is liberated. A settlement involving the former choice can take many forms. One of these is the creation of a separate Palestinian state in what became, in June 1967, occupied territory under Israeli military administration—namely, the West Bank and Gaza, the eastern and southern regions of Palestine that were annexed respectively by Jordan and occupied by the Egyptian military authorities in the first Arab-Israeli war in 1948.

° Both quotations occur in an interview which appeared in *Ha'aretz*, February 20, 1970, and are quoted in ibid., p. 42.

There are factors that lend force to the feasibility of this proposition. It is assumed that if the Palestinians accept this solution, the Zionists will at last have to pay the compensation for seized Palestinian land and property in Israel that the refugees have hitherto rejected; and it is also assumed that a land corridor along the Beersheba, connecting the West Bank to the Gaza Strip for access to the Mediterranean, would be granted. This would guarantee the economic and geographical viability of the projected state. The establishment of an entity such as this would be predicated in practice on the knowledge that a Palestinian nation is to be reborn, rather than an artificial state to be created.

Present Israeli insensitivity to the existence of the Palestinians and Hussein's mule-like stubbornness in trying to subdue them and their movement are hampering the efforts of Palestinian leaders to study, if only quietly, the conditions under which the idea of a separate, independent, and dynamic Palestinian state could evolve in reality.* It is quite obvious that a Palestinian state would give birth to the first truly popular government in the Arab world and be the first revolutionary regime in the area to represent the will of the people. For in contrast, the Iraqi, Egyptian, and other takeover governments in the Middle East came to power as an expression of nationalist or bourgeois movements rather than as a spontaneous explosion of the masses. The New Palestine nation will thus not be re-established for the benefit of rich landowners and businessmen, but for the working masses and the peasants.

The cohesiveness of Palestinian society, which has withstood nearly a quarter-century of stress and strain in exile and over fifty years of struggle for national determination, will be a great asset in generating the initial momentum for nationhood. The high literacy rate the Palestinians enjoy and the vast number of technicians

---

* The Israeli government has officially expressed its hostility to the idea of an independent state for the Palestinian people. "We do not believe," Golda Meir said (*Newsweek* interview, March 8, 1971), "there is room for three states between the Mediterranean and the Iraqi border . . . a third state is not possible if there is to be peace in the area . . ." In Amman the "parliament" condemned the notion of granting the Palestinians independence in any form (February 24, 1971).

and professionals they have would be an added advantage in the long-range development of the state. With independence, sovereignty, and dignity will come an understanding of the Zionist creation, just as with armed struggle, hope, and liberation an end came to bitterness, hate, and frustration. This state will present unlimited possibilities. The coexistence of a Palestine nation and an Israeli nation in the same region, with common borders, could lead to tentative contact between them. With the emergence of the newer generation of Israelis and Palestinians in the power structure of their respective states, a new dialogue is likely to ensue. A cultural, commercial, and social exchange between two peoples that are more alike in their fixations than any others, may result in an economic or even federal union. The liberation of Palestine will occur as a natural outgrowth of trust and gradual understanding.

At any rate, Palestinian leaders have not so far publicly endorsed the concept of a separate state and remain set in their aim of a return to Palestine and a secular state in place of the Zionist creation.

The establishment of a puppet Palestinian entity has also been envisaged, mostly by the Zionists and their friends in Amman. This advances the proposition of creating a semi-autonomous West Bank and Gaza, affiliated or in federation with Jordan or Israel. Efforts toward this got under way soon after the occupying forces moved into Palestinian territory in 1967. West Bank leaders ("West Bank notables" was the sobriquet that foreign correspondents often chose for them) were repeatedly approached for their approval. The Palestinians would obviously have gained nothing from such a dishonorable and degrading settlement, and as such it was rejected outright.

Should those elements in the Arab world, in Israel, and in the West continue to inhibit the realization of a national Palestinian expression, then the other, opposite, course open to us would be the intensification and perpetuation of armed violence, with its various possibilities and hazards.

One area of struggle involves Jordan. With its three-quarter Palestinian population, this country should in practice have a popular government. Hussein would have to go. He, along with his fun-loving family, his villas, fast cars, private planes, air-conditioned bowling alley, playboy gadgets, and his foreign advisers, could in time, be violently dislodged with the adoption of tactics accessible to guerrilla warfare, such as going underground and hitting at his throne attritionally. The accomplishment of this goal would enable the Palestinians to turn Jordan into a staging area for accelerated pressure on the Zionists and for consolidating their movement. In the occupied West Bank, strong cadres could be organized as a base for insurrection against the occupying forces. This would either be an open invitation for Israel to invade the East Bank or an open door for the first attempt from the Israeli side to recognize the rights of the Palestinian people.

The other, equally long-range, alternative left for the resistance movement would be to agitate for a series of upheavals in the Arab world in order to create the right revolutionary conditions for galvanizing the Arab masses and drawing them into the struggle. The overthrow of reactionary regimes in the Arab world and the appearance in their place of socialistically structured states ruled by the people would be a powerful buffer against Zionist diktats and Israeli rejection of the Palestinian entity. The dynamics of an Arab world actuated by a truly revolutionary consciousness would be a far cry from the feeble, nationalistic, and uncoordinated voice of Nasser-style pan-Arabism.

It is highly probable that, whatever the circumstances, the men and women who lead the Palestinian people would establish a government-in-exile similar to the one that grew from the Algerian Front de Libération Nationale and that existed during the guerrilla war against the French *colons*. Its recognition by world governments would strengthen the Palestinians' political base and lend credibility to their leaders as the official spokesmen of the Palestinian nation-in-exile. Ultimately, the various commando groups would merge, with their moderates and extremists meeting half way as the inevitable outcome of responsible political leadership.

The resistance is faced then by two perspectives on the road to liberation: one that sees a solution to our problem in our generation and another that dimly sees it, but sees it nevertheless, in our time as well as our sons' and probably their sons' time.

As a Palestinian, the prospect of an end to my isolation from the mainstream of other men's ordered activities and purposes exercises an intensely strange fascination on my mind. I am lured by the agony of wanting, *now*, in my own lifetime, the chance to know what it feels like, how the experience would sense in my brain, to be, for the first time since I was a child, the citizen of a country, a native of a land that is my own, all my own, with hills and mountains, and children in brick houses, where I could sit with my people, no longer menaced, no longer destitute.

I will not get this chance if some Arab leaders consider me a danger to their feudal systems and want to crush me, if some Israelis consider me nonexistent when I petition for my rights, and if the world considers me a mere refugee waiting for a shipment of food. Without this chance, I have nothing to lose. Everything to destroy. All the time to give.

This phase in the history of our people and revolution presents us with a challenge. How we respond to it is of crucial significance, not only to our national destiny but to our future as individuals and as an entity. The circumstances under which we face this challenge allow us no resort to half measures. We either look around us and soberly examine our aspirations and goals within the framework of our limitations, or are doomed to extend the helplessness and despair that characterized our existence for a quarter of a century as refugees and an exploited instrument in the hands of others. We are, in other words, confronted by the choice of a future as a nation-state or with destroying ourselves, like the long tormented Samson, by pulling down the pillars on ourselves and those around us.

We had a chance in 1937 and again in 1947 and, let us be honest, I say to my Palestinian brothers and sisters that we failed on both occasions essentially not because of what the colonialists and imperialists and Zionists and Arabs did to us but because of what we ourselves did not do. To enumerate these failures, to analyze the wrong steps we took, to blame our deprivations on the heavens or misfortune will not help us in this phase of our struggle. We performed badly at the test of history. We can do it again. Or we can face up to the challenge and transcend its boundaries.

We have, that generation of Palestinians whom I knew and to whom I related, with whom I grew up and suffered, with whom I groped for an identity and self-realization, with whom I shouldered the same bewilderment and anger, at this juncture in our lives, we have made remarkable gains. We have reminded the world that we exist (for so is the nature of reality inflected in our times that a man must nudge the world to remind it of one's existence) and that we exist as an independent people with a national identity. We have succeeded in speaking for ourselves; in speaking to those around the globe who are like us fighting to assert their sense of worth and purpose as human beings; in speaking about our cause in terms that others can understand; in speaking of our simple and earthly aspirations for a homeland. We have gained sympathy and approval for our dreams. We have fought and many of us have been killed for these dreams. We survived years of destitution to emerge as the most educated group in the Arab world, the only uncorrupted and progressive element in it; we established our credentials as a people motivated by an authentically revolutionary consciousness elevating itself above racism, hatred, and bitterness; and we are the vanguard of a movement that will actuate and enrich the Middle East.

But what can we do now? What lies ahead for us in this crucial phase of our revolution? The Egyptians have defected from our cause, or at least have reconsidered their priorities and concerns. The Jordanians want to crush us if they can. The Syrians and other Levantines want to reduce us to mere puppets and place us, as they had done before, under their erratic and irresponsible leadership. The Israelis have yet to acknowledge that we exist. The Big Powers want to put an end to us in one form or another. And we merely want to return to our homeland, to Palestine, where we and those already there can live in peace. Where we all belong.

But those who now rule and live in our homeland have not shown themselves susceptible to this solution. In a land where a poll shows 54 percent of the population hostile to the notion of giving up even occupied territory, let alone welcoming us back into their midst, we will have to do a devil of a lot more convincing than we have hitherto done. Or we have to intensify our armed struggle and match our words with violence. And this will mean we are setting for ourselves a goal the achievement of which will take not a year or two or three or a score, not a decade or two or three or a generation, not a lifetime or two or three, but it will take more. Maybe the shadow of infinity will loom ahead of us. Maybe we will perish on the road. Maybe, because we are human, we will make the same blunders we made before.

We know our rights in Palestine. There are many around the world who know our rights in Palestine. There are many more who one day will.

Can we wait?

Those reading this essay and those fifty thousand Palestinians with their arms and the dignity of freedom as they wait on the hills, and those of our people galvanized by truth, will say the response to this test should be positive. It is the whole we want and not the part. It is Palestine we want where we have our roots. It is not a New Nation we want if we have to plant them anew.

It was 1937. Then it was 1947. This was followed by 1971. We have paid a price. How much more can we pay?

If you live a comfortable existence where the problems of life are examined within the matrix of ideology and rationality, your world is a habitable one. If you give twenty years of your life in a refugee camp, you have paid a high price. If you are asked to sacrifice another twenty, the price becomes intolerable. If you are asked to make your yet unborn child take on your burden, you are committing an injustice. If you look around you and your existence is and has been a meaningless and tedious round of sparring with the vagaries of life for the most basic and the most simple needs of nature, when now you win, now you lose, ideology and rationality go out the mudhouse window into the courtyard, near the water pump, at the refugee camp. And because you are fatigued and dispossessed, you want to accept the part and not the whole. The Palestinian problem has never been to the Palestinian people a crisis, a crisis of political intent, but a tragedy, a tragedy they lived every day of their lives.

We are offered part of our homeland back; we have been robbed of the rest. We can examine the offer. We can bargain tenaciously. We can talk and reason and listen. We can look at what we have. What we have not. What we will have. If we can build a New Palestine nation where life will be meaningful and where we can lay the foundations for yet another era in self-assertion and rebirth in the short history of our revolution, when our revolutionary awareness can be coupled with evolutionary development, then we ought to commence now. If the New Palestine nation, before its inception, does not appear to truly represent our political aims, or will not truly be a projection of our dreams, then we reject it. Then we continue our struggle. Then we will have tried.

But let us not pass up our chance. Then, if circumstances continue to go against us, if hostile forces continue to oppress us and we fail, we will not be subjected to the indignity of harking back to the status quo ante, as the Arabs have done, and as the Palestinians did in 1937 and then again a decade later. For most of our growing-up years, the Arabs have looked at us and said: "To hell with you. Rot in your camps." Then they took custody of our cause and mutilated it, and us, beyond recognition. Now we can say to hell with them and regain custody, as we have done over the last few years, of our cause and determine its solution. Let the Arabs work on the liberation of, or negotiation over, Sinai and the Golan Heights. The Egyptians are entitled to adopt whatever modus operandi to get back a piece of desert and, in like manner, the Syrians can work out their own deal with the Israelis for the return of their mountain ridge.

That is an Egyptian and a Syrian concern. The fate of the West Bank, the Gaza Strip, Jerusalem, and the national destiny of the Palestinian people is an exclusively Palestinian concern. We operate on the logical assumption that the Israelis and those who back them understand this position. If they genuinely want peace, then their efforts toward it will be contingent on this knowledge, the knowledge that we are the only group in the area who can, or will be allowed to, negotiate it. We can give and expect concessions. We can see how sincere the Zionists are. We can examine the concept and then the feasibility of a sovereign Palestine state. We will do that not because we have no other options, but because we have. To work toward a favorable compromise is not to work toward a defeatist renunciation of our claims. I submit it is more in the nature of working toward averting the disaster of reliving the failures of our past. Our "defeatists" of the thirties and forties, who stopped for a breathing spell, for a moment of calm contemplation of the options open to them, are now hailed as the pragmatists. Will the "pragmatists" of the seventies, who in their frenzy sharpen the tragic dimensions of our dilemma, be hailed as the "defeatists"?

By advocating such a considerable shift from the point of departure of our national aims, I am haunted by an analogy that I find startling in its exactitude. We have owned and lived in a house from which we were evicted by force and which became occupied by a group of people stronger than us. After many years, we fail in our efforts to dislodge them; we fail in our efforts to receive justice from the court of law of the international community; we even fail in our efforts to return to live and share it with them. Now we are reduced to standing there, with hat in hand, looking down the bridges of our noses and asking to be allowed to settle in the backyard.

What will this mean to Palestinian pride, the Palestinian revolution, and the destiny of the Palestinian people? If we have no heart to doom ourselves to another generation of destitution, no right to doom our unborn children to a lifetime of violence, do we have the authority to take away from ourselves and from them the homeland in which we once lived? For by accepting the part and not the whole we are formally selling out our birthright and theirs and legitimizing the most blatant robbery in the history of modern times.

Our struggle, as we have proved, has not been merely to live in comfort, to pursue happiness, to acquire purpose, to create, to sing, to make love; it has not been merely to enrich our culture, to contribute to civilization, to leave our imprint on history. But it has been a struggle for the right to do it in Palestine. In the past we were repeatedly offered, were we not, the choice of resettlement elsewhere. More than Palestine, Syria has an abundance of cultivable land to till; Lebanon has more beautiful hills to build on; Australia a more developed economy to benefit from; other parts of the world a more splendid red carpet to welcome us on. But we opted to wait for a return to our homeland, where we had lived, where we danced the dabke, played the oud, where the men wore their checkered hattas and the women their embroidered shirts, where the sun shone in the winter and the smell of oranges permeated the air and the soul.

How could we have conveyed this agony of yearning to the Big Powers and the Big World, long used to treating us for the natives we were? "Natives"—a term for which they devised a special definition. We were the natives of the land whose past fate was subject to the whims of Western cigar-smoking cabinet ministers. Dispossessed natives of the land whose present fate others have tried to manipulate in the West and the East. The Big Four (and I swear to heavens this is what they are called) discuss methodically what they are going to do with us. The imperialist world wants to destroy us, for we pose a threat to their oil interests, and their aircraft, and their trade routes. And those miserable specimens of leadership, the Arab statesmen, want to tell us what to do.

The Egyptians, we hear, "demand back" the Gaza Strip. They do not even pretend to demand it back in the name of the Palestinian people. They want to reoccupy it, impose the previous military administration, and have us trade one master for another. The Jordanian "parliament" passes a motion to "refuse" the establishment of a separate Palestinian state. In other words, we are witnessing a process designed to strip us of our very basic right to decide our own future. Where do we turn? Do we, as some in our own family have advocated, view our struggle as a long, long one indeed and attempt to revolutionize the Arab world behind us? And then, strong, organized, and determined, turn outward and impose our own diktat on an intransigent enemy? Or do we, still others in our own family have argued, bargain for the establishment of a viable independent Palestinian state? We are thus apprehensive on the one hand that the ruthless power of the imperialist reactionary world would defeat us in the attempt, uncertain on the other hand of whether, by compromising, we are compromising our rights and abdicating our revolutionary role. If we ultimately opt for the former, the challenge is great. If we opt for the latter, the challenge is greater.

In the creation of a Palestinian state there will be many questions to answer. And I do not speak here of boundaries determining whether the state will incorporate Transjordan, how Gaza and the West Bank are to be joined, access to the Mediterranean, the status of Jerusalem, economic and geographic viability, and so on. I speak here of the ability of this state to emerge as a true expression of the Palestinian consciousness and as a culmination of the true will of the Palestinian people. The test will lie also in how genuinely it can reflect itself as a spokesman for those Palestinians living in Israel, and those Palestinians who may continue living in other parts of the world. For if it fails, it will fail as Israel has failed in its attempt to distinguish itself as an extension of the humanist and liberal traditions of Jewishness. In that event, we will have struggled and suffered in vain.

We have gone a long way. We can go further. In a way, I say to my Palestinian brothers and sisters, most of our growing-up years have been a preparation for our inevitable revolution and liberation. We have all been involved in this revolution, this fight for liberation. All of us have taken part in it and no doubt will continue to do so. There are those of us who were engaged in guerrilla warfare, those who endangered their lives to hit back at the imperialist and in an infinitesimally small way contribute to the destruction of his capitalist world, those who returned from wherever they had been around the globe to offer their services as doctors, teachers, and organizers at the camps, those who, in one form or another, gave of themselves to the cause. Whether we gave two hours of our time at a free clinic, two lira of our money in the collection box, or two smacks across the earhole to someone who called us a two-bit Palestinian, we were of and in the revolution. We cannot go back now. We cannot be defeated now. But we can fail if we are not strong enough to want to see the options open to us and relate our future goals to our past accomplishments.

The altered conditions in the focus of the Arab-Israeli conflict, coupled with the shift in emphasis on the fear the Arabs had of the ultimate designs of "the Zionist enclave in the Arab heartland," may expand our opportunities rather than inhibit them. During the next few years, or it could be the next few months, the Palestinian revolution and the Palestinian people will be called upon to assert their political dynamism, their independence, and their responsibility. In this lies the challenge to us. In this our battle for liberation will be won or lost.

In a way, all that I have written on the preceding pages is really a journal. My own and the journal of thousands of Palestinians like myself who grew up in the Middle East over the last two decades. I have written it to satisfy myself and those who want to know that our struggle has not been merely for a place in the sun and a standard of living, but a struggle for dignity and national identity. That which has been taken away from us was not only our homeland; that which has been given to us was not only destitution. From us was taken a part of our essence as human beings, and in return we received the desperation of a void, a negation. I want to regain that essence of my worth as a human being, to reclaim it from a time:

—When I and my people are dismissed contemptuously within quotation marks.

—When the problem of our diaspora will be solved only by those who wish to endorse international funds and loans and indemnities for our resettlement.

—When every day I walk down the muddy paths of refugee camps.

—When every year old men die burdened with memories. And children, who did not know, began to hate.

—When I took a group of suntanned Westerners, by force, to that edge of the desert where I lived and grew up for twenty-three years. Where they found it uncomfortable for a few days.

Where they could not remember that it was the home they had given us to live in, sitting up on our knees.

—When the world condemns me because I decided to sit up and lift my head and declare my right to cultivate the potential around me for happiness and purpose.

—When I got tired of slogans, theirs and ours.

—When I got tired of the Israelis and the Arabs, of the Big Powers and their games and clients and pronouncements and resolutions and conferences and releases and statements. I also got tired of those who wanted us to be the people who should have melted into history, never to return, like the cloud formation poised in the sky that was destroyed by a storm, never to be seen again.

My father died burdened with question marks from his past that he carried around him like a tired old beast of burden pulling at a heavy cart. I am beginning to acquire a past of my own that is itself getting onerous. But if they think I am resigned to it, I ask them to remember that my background has given me enough traumas and hangups to come out of my ears. I suspect one of these may be arson. I could put a match to this whole world if they are not careful, and I may do it while they are busy debating my problem at the UN, putting my name in parentheses, sending me a shipment of their lousy food, and expecting me, the slave of their fucked-up power politics, to be in love with my chains.

I do not belong to, recognize, or relate to that age, so recent in history, when strong men ruled over weak ones; when a handful of nations felt it their right to dissect the world into colonies and spheres of economic exploitation; when a garrison of freckle-nosed, fat-bellied army officers lorded it over the wogs and the chinks and the gypos and the gooks and the bicots; when His Majesty's government, or somebody else's wretched government, deemed it a cultural and social favor to impose its presence on other people's soil and choose for them their place in history and their fate in life.

If you belong to that age and are a member of that generation of men, then let me tell you where I am. Mine are different times, with a different tempo and a different structure of concerns. I am not taking a repeat performance from you or anyone else. My father did, when you went to him with your traditions of cruelty and violence, your beliefs in the inherent superiority of your race, and killed him, and many like him around the globe, shrugging over their bodies and their fragmented beings. We are not taking it on the chin from you or anyone else. In these times of ours we have intentions of giving it. What do we lose? What do we have? Our roles around the world as pariahs, as ignoble savages, as coolies, as street people, as hewers of wood and drawers of water? Our poverty, our hunger, our pain? Your gifts of miracle rice and foreign aid and the wonders of technology and the standards of your rotting society?

You thought it never did matter with a native. You probably still do. But if you come to me—as an agent of your generation and times—with that swagger, with that arrogant sniff on your pimply face that was well known and feared from Calcutta to Singapore, from Trinidad to Rhodesia, don't come too close. I might blow your brains out before you get a chance to utter your usual, "Move on nigger, move on wog!"

In my early teens I grew weary as I sat around Beirut shaay shops. Now in my late twenties I grow impatient as I sit in London libraries articulating my convictions and narrating my grievance. I pore over books that argue the problem of my people and the conditional in their history—"if" they had stood up to fight, "if" they had been united, "if" they had preferred death in their homeland to a diaspora in another, "if" they had been wise to their roles as pawns in the hands of Arab benefactors, "if" they had been as vicious as their adversaries had been vicious. And so on. But I cannot relate to these imponderables. I am not my brother's keeper, nor am I accepting the legacy of fatalism and humble pie that he bequeathed to me.

I pore over books that give me claims and counter-claims to the land of Palestine. Who gives two piasters about all this khara anyhow? I am not going to relate to a scholar's abstract thesis about my own homeland and my own consciousness. I could not even relate to my own father who lived out his last years in exile, mumbling incoherencies he had overheard on Radio Cairo, clutching, like the drowning man he was, at straws that floated on the surface of his troubled life from UN debates and speakers' platforms.

As we grew weary in our teens of racist obscenities spouted off behind microphones and of mouths shooting off draconian threats, we grow more confirmed now that our station in life is not our tent in a refugee camp; that our place in the world is not one of continued exile; that our position among men is not one of duress; that our demands from the world are not for monetary compensation and integration in host countries. We grow more confirmed that our dignity and our destiny are not for sale.

What manner of people were we taken for by the Western and the Arab world? Were we to remain forever the sons of Tantalus? The news in yesterday's newspaper? The word within quotations in somebody's mediocre book? The men arrested in their climb up the steep mountain of history, there to remain, unable to ascend, to descend, soon to blend with the inanimate rock and vanish from the sight of those above, those below?

How long can the Zionists continue to live in their Promised Land, in our homeland, with inflexible sensibilities and flexed muscles, poised for the defense of their conquest and diktat over us? How can they continue to retard the revolution in human morality with their "rampart of Europe," their "outpost of civilization," their "Jewish state"? How can they bring the vices and follies of racism, expansionism, occupation, and annexation from an age in the past that condoned them to an age in the present that condemns them?

I sit here and read articles and books and quotations and I listen to commentaries and debates that want to prove to *me* that I am not really a Palestinian. I am a "southern Syrian," an Arab who moved from one part of the Arab world to the other with the impressive ease of a commuter going from the Bronx to Brooklyn, or from Grenoble to the *cinquième* in Paris. They want to convince *me* that I really had no national consciousness as a Palestinian; that my emotional fixation on Palestine was misplaced; that my homeland was just a "wasteland" before the hardworking Zionists got there. And what the hell, why couldn't a "southern Syrian" live in northern Syria anyhow?

I say I am tired of quotations and polemics written by scholars and researchers for each other, to delineate how the conflict originated, how it developed, how it will be settled. The conflict is between the Arabs and the Israelis, they write. It is between the Egyptians and the Jews. It is between Palestinians and Zionists. It is between one national movement and another national movement. It is between this and that.

Who gives a khara? I don't want to be convinced, nor do I want to be informed, what my problem is by sociologists with their methodological charts, social scientists with their historical documents, or commentators with their definitive quotations.

They can explain to me that I have no rights in Palestine, that I am a southern Syrian or an Arab or whatever damn name they choose for me, till they are blue in the face, and I will read it till my eyeballs pop out, but they cannot explain to me the causes of my existential discontent.

The role I played in the tragedy of the Palestinian people was one in a cast of over two million, but it distorted my mind. The way the tragedy was directed and produced embittered my being. When the Six Day War broke out, pitting Arabs against Israelis, I was in India and had been away for three years. But with my consciousness stuffed up with frustration and my head with hashish, I hoped the ben sharmootas would destroy each other. What difference would it have made to me to trade one military administration for another? What difference would it have made who the aggressor, who the victim, was? The Egyptians ruled over us in Gaza, and the Arabs in the Levant, as badly as the Zionists ruled over our brothers and sisters in occupied Palestine.

It was as though the Arabs and the Israelis were fighting over a cause that no longer concerned me. It was as if I had been robbed even of my sense of perspective as I detachedly contemplated, in my nether-nether land, the six days of a war that was being waged in another nether-nether land. I was suspended aloft, outside and beyond the conflict. Having been reduced to a zero, a naught in the scheme of things, I was incapable of reaching a decision about my position in the mathematics of the conflict. I was also, at that stage in my depravity, incapable of mustering either repugnance at Arab threats to kill, rape, and "drive them into the sea," or anger at Israeli designs for expansion and subjugation. All my reserves of anger and repugnance had long been dissipated at other times, at other places.

Then it came about that we could not wait to be freed, and we broke out. With freedom from bondage came freedom of the spirit. Came humanity. A return to pride. A feeling of our place. A defiance. An exhilaration. A wonder. An awakening. A rebirth. Came a certainty that we were not the wretched natives of the earth. That we were not alone. That we had brothers and sisters fighting in Vietnam, in Africa, in South America, in the United States and elsewhere. That we were together. We were in the same battle. Against the same enemy. For the same cause. The battle, the enemy, and the cause are the same when I fight against an Arab for the Kurdish people's rights; when the Kurd fights against a Zionist for the Palestinian people's rights.

I returned from my retreat in the East and went up on the rooftops to shout to the world that I was a Palestinian. I was no longer alone, hiding, shamefaced, embittered. I belonged to a people who shared their travails and their accomplishments with a commonwealth of men and women across the world who like them struggled to remove the leaf covering the nakedness of imperialist oppression. I was a Palestinian and the name had a cadence to it. I was not the bewildered, wretched native of the land; I was the native son.

The realization of who I was, the belief in the justice of my cause, came to me not because I viewed it in the framework of politics and ideology, but because I sensed it in the very fabric of my soul. The complexities and cabalas of dialectical reasoning neither diminished nor enhanced my belief, my knowlege, my awareness.

The process leading to the Palestinian revolution and the rehumanization of the Palestinian psyche indeed came about long before the emergence of the Palestinians as a politicized and militant nucleus in the Arab world. It occurred in our minds before the armed struggle began. We commenced in our teens to question the hitherto accepted assumptions, reject the refugee mentality that our elders had acquired, and even discard the patterns of our cultural makeup.

As an unconscious manifestation of our disenchantment, for example, we shocked our parents by refusing to adhere to the social dictates that governed the observation of the Eid. At a time of the year when, traditionally, Palestinians go around dressed in their best attire and visit friends and relatives to celebrate the Eid, we opted to ostentatiously wear our grubbiest clothes and head to the beaches. At a time in the late fifties when our parents were in dire need of recalling the exploits of national heroes, we ridiculed these and their memories. The more they turned to find a refuge in the old ways, the more we turned away to seek the creation of new ones. The holier the concept was to them, the less worthy it was to us. As their resignation increased, our anger mounted. We grew up in a vacuum. We belonged to no nation. We embraced no culture. We were at the bottom. The only way for us to go was up.

If the object of our dissatisfaction stemmed from a desire to protect ourselves against abuse and degradation, and the style of our social and family system was conducive to perpetuating them, then our unrest could not be channeled and dissipated within the established order. If the cause of our dissatisfaction was the reluctance the world had for listening to our grievance and the contempt with which it treated us, then we hit back at the world. And to hell with the ben sharmootas. We had nothing to lose. We lived on the edge of the desert. On the fringe of the world. We had little to risk. We were too miserable to inflict further hardship and further pain on ourselves.

We made common cause with the oppressed. The oppressors made common cause against us. The revolution of the Third World will succeed even if it fails. "No revolution is ever lost, however abortive," Ralph Roeder says in his biography of Benito

Juarez, "no reform ever fails completely. Its results may be abolished but . . . the movement returns pendulum-wise by the momentum of the reaction."

The armed struggle of the Palestinian people may continue for decades and the end may not be in sight; but its outcome is foretold. That is the way I know it. That is the way I feel it in my senses.

Epilogue 1974

Epilogue 1974

When the Munich incident occurred, resulting in the death of
eleven Israeli athletes, two Palestinian commandos and one
German policeman, it received wide and often sensational
coverage in the Western establishment press. How the average
Palestinian related to the incident—coming as he did from the
kind of world that he had inhabited—might best be summed
up in my own reflection at the time, which was: I do not
understand. I do not understand how in the midst of all the
hysterical indignation and all the vociferous language no one
seemed to be aware that the Munich construct of violence, in

its institutional but blatantly overt form, was at that same moment being practiced against many Palestinians under occupation, as it was against many other Third World peoples.

I still do not understand. Maybe I never will. How can I be expected to understand that innocent people live only in the West? That the victims of violence become tragic figures only if they are of European stock? That concentration camps are acceptable in Gaza but barbaric anywhere else? That 13,000 Palestinian prisoners can languish in Israeli jails, but are refused access to the Red Cross and become victim to the most primitive methods of torture, while the cause of sixty-three Israelis in Syrian jails is transformed into a problem of the utmost concern for the Western community? How can I be expected to understand the notion that those who colonize and occupy and napalm somehow acquire a higher moral authority to inflict violence on us because it is institutional and is accompanied by pious claims?

The construct of Palestinian violence has roots in private terrors contained in that encapsulated world of non-being to which Palestinians have been relegated and still inhabit after twenty-five years. Indeed, a world where voices were silenced whenever they were raised, and heads were hit whenever they were lifted.

The private terrors that shadow the everyday life of the exile, the refugee, the occupied, the stateless would have forever remained private were it not for the fact that from these terrors an occasional outcry of fathomless anger is emitted, spilling over to the outside world. This outside world, standing with its back to the human passions housed within the confines of the ghetto, the refugee camp, the occupied city, and the colonized town, does not understand these occasional outcries, simply because their idiom and their metaphor, their cause and effect stem from a reality alien to the outside world. Yet those of us who have known no other reality, driven by it as if by the terrors of a primal pain, also share our humanity with other men and women, denying them monopoly of this humanity.

Such is the matrix of logic of the outside world in this day that the onus always falls on the oppressed to explain his position, to prove his sincerity, to justify his platform, to articulate his vision of the future and to truly, truly convince his oppressor (whose napalm and military occupation, whose racist excesses and sadistic regressions have crushed his very soul and reduced him to a fragment) that he is motivated by love and not hate. Above all, he is called upon to believe in the notion that the violence of the oppressor to subdue him with sophisticated weapons and keys to the dungeons, is moral. His own violence which he uses to break his chains is immoral. And so on.

When the Munich incident occurred, I was living in Paris. I had chosen Paris primarily because I was stateless, and a stateless person chooses a city because it happens to be less hostile to him at that time than others; say Beirut, where I had grown up. In Paris I lived with my wife in the Fourteenth Arrondisement. The police came to see us there. They were kind enough to address us as monsieur and madame and to leave my wife alone. (Whether the fact that she is an American citizen had anything to do with it, no one can say.) They even asked if I would be *willing* to come to the police station to answer a few questions. Other Palestinians—students, intellectuals and activists—were similarly approached and questioned, either at their homes or at the Prefecture de Police. Among them was a friend of mine from the General Union of Palestinian Students. I complained to him about the indignity of it and suggested that this might be a good time to organize, to keep the situation from getting out of hand, as it did in Germany and Holland where hundreds of Arabs were being jailed or deported. He said this indignity was nothing compared to what our people were subjected to, particularly on the West Bank and Gaza. I thought the remark was too theatrical at a time like this, but I let it pass. He said he was not afraid of the French police. He was not afraid of anything—except deportation to Jordan, whose passport he was carrying. If I am sent there that will be the last anyone will ever hear from me, and I can not imagine anything to be more afraid of, he says.

I do not know what *I* was afraid of. I had nothing to hide and nothing, theoretically, to fear; but that is not the way it works when you are a Palestinian. There are special laws, as if devised specifically for you, to govern your movements. And you have no consul to appeal to, no senator to whom you can write. No legal or moral rules that protect you at a moment of crisis.

I was questioned twice, on two separate occasions; and each time, innocuously enough, the questions dealt with the nature of my activities, source of income, the identity of my friends, and other related issues. It was all put in a file, I noticed, marked Palestine. (It was gratifying to know that the French at least recognized our existence, unlike those who were raising very serious doubts about the professional skills of their optometrists by saying that we did not.)

I was questioned again and again—whenever Palestinians hijacked a plane or indulged in an act of violence. Each time I was let go by the police because I could not help them with their inquiries. And each time I would reflect on how appropriate it was that I, though having no connection with these acts, should have been questioned by the authorities. For were these acts of violence also not my own violence, a projection of my own upbringing, the product of an experience that I have shared with a whole generation of Palestinians? I would leave the police station and walk the streets of Paris—no longer strange to me as all European cities are by now no longer strange to me—engulfed by the tension of a space all my own. Of course I knew what Palestinian violence was all about. Of course I knew, in a sense, every one of those men and women whom the world was calling "murderers" and "international outlaws." I grew up with them, and even in my isolation here in this city, I knew how they had felt. Was I not, at various moments in my own life, at unguarded moments in recent years, as currents of frustration gripped my soul, as I choked and there was no place to run for air, driven into wanting to disabuse myself of my sense of perspective and use the only power of which I had not been robbed, my power to use violence? And did I not come closer to it than I care to admit?

In the summer of 1973 I make an effort to "return to the countries." "The countries" is a phrase that a Palestinian uses when he means he wants to "go back home," that is to say to any of the countries in the Arab world where his family happens to be living. I have not been to the countries for a number of years, so I buy a ticket to fly from Paris to Beirut. At the airport I line up with other passengers at customs and immigration. I am holding on to my travel document, an Australian passport that I had acquired during my long stay in Australia. It says on it I was born in Haifa, Israel. Maybe the Australian authorities were not aware that when I was born Israel had not come into existence. The immigration official looks at me and looks at my passport. He reads my name aloud. Maybe he has heard of me, since some of my work has been translated into Arabic. Soon he is going to smile at me and wish me a pleasant stay in his country.

"Are you an Israeli," he says with horror.

"No! I am a Palestinian."

He points to my passport and tells me that it says Israel there. I tell him that although Australians believe I was born in Haifa, *Israel*, he and I know that I was born in Haifa, *Palestine*. He wants to know if I have been there in recent months. I say no, I have not returned since the exodus of 1948.

I do not know how to explain to him, or anyone else, in my own way, that of course I have returned to Palestine, that I have been there every day of my life and that I have recreated it in my mind, in its entirety, and let it govern the structure of my everyday concerns. And that I have carved it out in all these alien lands where I have lived over the last twenty-five years.

Another official argues with me for a full hour and says, in essence, that although he was convinced that I was a Palestinian, my identity makes it all the more reason that the Deuxième Bureau investigate me. (They even use a French name for their security system.) And I stand there as French tourists go through, Italian nuns go through, American businessmen go through, Israeli spies go through, and the whole world goes through. Then I am made to wait in the Transit Lounge till the next day. I gag with anger and indignation. Violent thoughts rock my being at the knowledge that I had deluded myself into thinking that our reality had changed in recent years, that it had become less painful and less degrading.

Next morning someone tells me with an impatient wave of the hand that I should get ready to return to France on the next available Middle East flight. I say I am buying a ticket on any other airline except that. The gendarme who accompanies me around the airport wants to sell me hashish or to buy him liquor and cigarettes from the duty free shop. When I ask him if he would let me use a phone to ring up my family, he says he cannot break the law.

Before I get on the plane, an official with a file under his arm tells me that I don't say nice things about the Arab regimes, do I? I say I don't, do I? I don't have anything nice to say about anyone.

In Paris I become preoccupied with the thought that our condition has not changed in any way; we are still fair game for abuse. I become possessed with it. I walk around the city, brooding over it. My mind thinks about nothing else. I think about nothing other than the fact that everything that happens to me, that happens to us, as individuals and as a nation, stems from our political condition. I begin to have fantasies about what I should have done. I begin to think that perhaps our lives are not worth living like this. Perhaps we are better dead than alive. I begin to think about killing the Lebanese consul in Paris. I become slowly mad, pathologically insane. I receive a letter from home telling me that my mother has gone nearly blind from crying over the incident. "But do not worry, my son," the letter adds. "We shall soon return to our homeland."

My murderous zeal dissipates itself. Before it does, I had already spoken with impassioned sincerity to friends about attacking the Lebanese consul, shooting him down, blowing up his car, and about other weird plans I had bristling in my head, stunning me with their sense of urgency. I was aware that what I intended to do was not to help anybody's cause but my own, by projecting it into a statement of violence whose idiom stemmed from my situation as the citizen of a whole nation in exile that continues to be occupied, mortified and inflicted with violence.

An elderly Palestinian friend of mine, who had lived in Paris since her expulsion from the West Bank by the occupying authorities, came to me in a panic. She assailed me immediately. "What the hell is the matter with you? What are you trying to do?" And what good would it be for our people's cause, she wanted to know, if I killed someone at the Lebanese Embassy. I said it would do the cause no good at all. "But it would make *me* feel good," I added flippantly. In later weeks I came to think that there was more to that remark, and more to my attempt to indulge in violence, than the flippancy I had expressed to my friend.

I wanted to feel "good." I wanted to feel no longer inferior and helpless; I wanted to rid myself of the feeling that I was not a determining force in my life. I wanted to remove from my body and from my soul the grime of my refugeeism, statelessness, submissiveness, and the grime that was the blurred, degrading image that others had acquired of sense of humanity. I wanted to confront those who denied my existence and the notion that I (as if I were a different species of man) could not feel pain. I wanted to stand face to face with those people and demand that they look in my eyes and see their own humanity reflected there.

The psychological or cathartic function of the idea that I could confront the Lebanese consul (or his Israeli or American counterpart, had the situation so demanded) stemmed from a deep need within my being, and not from a marginal side of my experience, it stemmed, as it were, from the mosaic of my active mythology as a Palestinian and the whole range of my human existence.

My reality as a Palestinian, the total collage of graphic

images that I carry in my consciousness as an Arab, is derived from a process of violence. Violence that was inflicted on me every day of my life and the life of a whole generation of Palestinians till we grew up with it like we grew up with our skin. Made inert by my condition, all that I am left with, all that is open for me is to face up to those who negate my birth right and human right. Confronting them and their system, on any level, as an individual or with a group, is the true link to my past. Success in this confrontation is my quintessential future. The transmutations of value around which the foundation of Palestinian society (or any other Third World society) is erected will always remain alien to a Westerner. His concerns and ours are, literally, worlds apart. We are motivated by a collective motion/energy born of the feeling that our everyday lives are interlaced with the perception of history and its workings. Whichever way we turn, there is a delicate correlation between political and existential realities. Our quality of hope, the reservoir of our turbulent energy and the vehemence of consciousness are an existential concern; but when these go bad in the teeth, it is because of our political situation. The lofty issues of restructuring one's integrity and reassembling one's past become every individual's milieu. For try as you will, try as often as you might, to escape your reality, your identity, your Self, yet it follows you every hour, every day of your life —that incessant logic showing you how, with your history deflected from its preordained course, there is no rest for you until you have regained that intangible and exquisite tool which men and women use to identify themselves as spiritual beings and of which you have been robbed. Only then will you begin to become concerned with the down-to-earth issues that characterize the existence of other people.

Coming so close to committing an act of pure violence as I did in the summer of 1973 in Paris, frightened me, because I was reminded that the violence of Black September—and I submit that the name connotes a construct of violence (rather than an organized group) that grew out of the bloody events in

Jordan and the foreign occupation in the West Bank and Gaza
—is also my own violence; that had I been exposed to a series
of stimuli, enough pain ånd sufficient doses of torture to my
body and soul as other Palestinians had, I would have been
capable and ready to kill and destroy as they had. When I recall the restless twenty-five years I have spent in the ghourba,*
desperately searching for human and political resolutions to
our problem, I can not conjure up one halcyon period, one
cloudless summer, when my existence was not characterized by
violence whose nature, whose effect on the human spirit,
was not more devastating than any form of physical violence.

A Palestinian's sensitivity to injustice and his response to it
has roots in his private situation as a third-class citizen in
Israel, as a man or a woman living under military occupation in
the West Bank and Gaza, as the denizen of a refugee camp in
Jordan, Lebanon, and Syria, and as a person robbed of his
patrimony who must acquire a tough veneer merely to survive.
Against him is a system, a force, denying his existence, assuring
his continued frustration and erecting around him blackened
walls where existence can not achieve a normal or full pitch of
reality.

Palestinian violence does not occur in a vacuum. It is best
understood in the dichotomy that exists between the oppressor
and the oppressed, the occupier and the occupied, the colonizer
and the colonized, the master and the slave; the violence used
by the master to subdue his slave and the violence of the slave
to break his chains. If there are limits to be placed on the use
of violence—be it revolutionary violence, terroristic violence,
individualistic violence, or adventurist violence—then there
are, in like manner, equal limits to be placed on the capacity
of men and women to absorb pain, suffering, and degradation.

---

* Palestinian diaspora. For an understanding of how Palestinians in the
early years after their expulsion from Palestine came to view their stay in
host countries 'and the concept of the ghourba and Awda (Return), see
A. L. Tibawi, "Visions of the Return: The Palestine Refugees in Arab
Poetry and Art," *Middle East Journal* (Fall 1963), pp. 507–26.

From the promotion of the racist concept that we, in the desolation of our world, can somehow be made "meek," comes the leading myth that you can spit on the soul of defeated peoples, reduce them to a fragment and not expect a response.

Paris during, before, and after the events in Jordan in the black month of September 1970, was a stopping place for various Palestinian individuals on their way to and from the Middle East. These transients "from the countries" would be students going to England for their tertiary education, immigrants heading to the United States, affluent Palestinian-Americans going to the Arab world for a visit, mechanics, shopkeepers, peasants, and youngsters from the West Bank seeking employment on the Continent, and poets, writers, and editors from Jerusalem traveling back and forth from Palestine, the Arab world, and Europe as if contacting other Palestinians not living under occupation had some mystical, healing effect. Meeting them, and talking to them at length, reinforced my feeling that the Palestinian Arab experience is a strikingly cogent one that cuts across class lines (expulsion from Palestine and its effect on one's national psyche had not been the lot of only a specific socioeconomic class); but more than that, I became aware of the terror and the violence that Palestinians must submit to under occupation. And I would ask, repeatedly, incredulously, but my God, is that what it is really like? I feel a chilling sensation gripping my being; and when I have listened to it all, in a lull in the conversation I would feel anger, incredible anger that we should have become so helpless, so destitute. People tell me stories and some narrate them with the sigh of resignation that has come to rule over their lives and their affairs. Some do so with bitterness. But the rest talk to me with passion and with self-confidence about the future and an assured sense of their place in it.

The deportations, the blowing up of homes, the expropriation of property, the arrogance on the faces of Israeli soldiers walking into Arab coffee shops in Jerusalem to slap the patrons on the face and demand identity cards, and the primitive tor-

ture of members of the resistance*—all these go on, and to
the outside world "the Arabs" have never had it so good. Look
at how our standard of living is better than ever. We earn excellent wages under occupation. We drive cars. We watch
television. Our health standards have improved. And they show
pictures of our West Bank "notables," our Uncle Toms and our
Beni oui oui, as if to attest to this, shaking hands with Israeli
military governors. And nobody seems to realize that, during
all this, Palestinians called and fought for a secular state and
not for a struggle to inflict on Israeli society the same devasta-
tion they inflicted on us.

I begin to lose my patience and my sense of rationality. I
begin to feel that our lives are not worth living anywhere in
this world, anywhere. It is impossible for me to be oblivious of
my situation; to be, as it were, happy. Moments of gloom and
fury overwhelm my being as I spend restless days in Paris
and I see pictures of robust Israelis tilling our land, growing our
oranges, inhabiting our cities and towns, co-opting our culture, and talking in their grim, stubborn way about how we do
not "exist" and how our country was a "desert" before they
went there. And I gag with anger and mortification.

I no longer physically live in the place we had set out from.
Yet I very much live there, because this place is no longer
just a mere geographical entity, but my idiom, my ethos, my
laughter. I no longer care to explain anymore. I am just
sustained by the belief that we have *survived* and prevented

---

* According to the Israeli newspaper, *Maariv*, in a report published
May 3, 1971, ". . . 5620 Arabs have been sentenced in the Gaza strip
alone for life imprisonment and hard labor; among prisoners there are
men over 80 years old and children between 12–14 years of age." Wide-
spread use of the most extreme and ugly forms of torture have been practiced against these prisoners and others, on the West Bank and inside
Israel. See International Committee of the Red Cross, *Report* (December 5,
1968), U.N. Working Group, U.N. Document E/CN. 4/1016/add. 2
(February 11, 1970), and particularly Amnesty International in its report on Israeli methods of torture (April 1970).

repeated attempts to do away with our identity. I am sustained by the knowledge that our continued existence, in the face of all this, has become an existential statement about human beings and their capacity to suffer, to endure, to survive and to fight.

So I just sit in Paris and I write and speak, convincing myself that what I am doing is work for the cause of our people. I measure my life in the fragments of time I spend with my fellow expatriates who have newly arrived in the city. One of these is a youngster from Nablus who is ten years my junior. He is known by the nickname Kamous (dictionary), probably because he is fluent in many languages. His concerns revolve around Kamal Nasser, the Palestinian poet and member of the Resistance. He knows by heart every line of poetry Nasser has written and he infuses each with a mystical significance that somehow escapes me. Kamous floats around France, indeed around Europe, without a passport or identity papers of any kind. He is forever getting into confrontations with the French whom he despises. He is forever angry with himself and with the world. The year before, when he had finished his studies in Germany, he tried to go back home to Nablus.

So I go to the Israeli embassy, he says, and I apply for a permit—the *Israeli* embassy for God's sake. I go to the *Israeli* embassy to ask for a *permit* to go back to *my* home. But to hell with it. I go. When I tell them what I want they say they can only grant me a visitor's visa. I say they can't do that—I am a Palestinian, I was born there, it's my country they're talking about giving me a visitor's visa for. And they give me a dirty look and say they can do whatever the hell they please. I try to reason with them. They drag me out.

Kamous gesticulates with his arms as he speaks. His voice rises and falls to accentuate his arguments. He mimics the accent and the mannerisms of the people he is talking about. There is so much verbal violence all around him.

So I go back, he continues. I go back to the Israeli embassy and tell them I am agreeable; if all they'll give me is a visitor's visa, so be it. It seemed as though there was nothing I could do about it at that point except to pray that the curse of all the prophets befall them and crush them as they have crushed us. Before I return to Palestine, I go through Lebanon, Syria, and Jordan. Like every Palestinian family, mine is fragmented all over. When I cross the Bridge, the Israeli police pick me up, probably because I gave them a lot of lip and because they thought I looked suspicious, whatever that means in their book.

At the station I continue to protest my innocence and they put me in a room whose mere sight terrifies me. It looks so macabre with broken chairs heaped up in a corner, a horribly filthy jacket on the floor with mold on it, and bloodstains on one of the walls. I sit on a chair and opposite me, on another, sits this fellow from the Shin Bet and I tell you they're the most sadistic mob of animals in the world. I begin to protest my innocence. He lifts his foot, puts it between my legs and leaves it there. I ask him what he is doing that for. As if in response, he pushes it hard down on my testicles. He wants to know who my "connections" or "contacts" are in Lebanon and Syria. And every time I say I have no connections and made no contacts in these countries, he pushes his boot down again.

You know what we ought to do, Kamous asks me with intense passion, almost rising from his chair, you know what we ought to do? He tells me that when we are ultimately liberated, we ought to form a squad, a special squad, to hunt down these individuals and bring them in to stand trial in front of a revolutionary court.

At night, in my cell, I try to sleep and that is all I can think about: these barbarians have to be stopped. Every two hours or so, someone walks in—probably the guard or whoever the hell he was—bangs open the door, grabs me by the throat, flashes a knife at me and walks out. Can you see that?

They take me to court and ask the judge to allow them to hold me under preventive detention. It's a ten-minute operation, but that's all it takes to keep someone they don't like, an activist or potential activist, out of circulation for as long as they want. In court everybody is speaking Hebrew. I don't understand much of their damn language, but enough to follow the proceedings. I feel like maybe I ought to shout at them in my own language, shoving my own name and the name of my country down their throats till it burns them to a cinder; but I feel so exhausted and helpless. What saves me that day, indeed what saves me from becoming insane over the next thirteen months (a fate that befell so many hundreds of prisoners like me) was what I saw happening in court in the case that came up for trial before mine. An old man is standing before the judge, a West Banker with a thick mop of grey hair and a mustache. He is talking to the judge as I walk into the courtroom. The judge is asking him if he does not feel remorse now that his house had been blown up. The old man, anecdotally, tells him he feels no remorse at all. Indeed he feels gratification that his house had been blown up. The judge asks him to explain why that is so. The man says he has been paid for the loss twice over. Why, asks the judge, this European judge sitting in our courts, in our country, passing sentence on our affairs. The West Banker tells him that he and his family feel amply compensated because his son is in the Resistance movement and that, on a visit home once, he told his father that he and his comrades had shot down an Israeli helicopter. You have blown up my house, but I was paid in advance, do you see?

Before they lock me up in the Nablus jail for the next eleven months, I get the usual treatment of beatings, banging a door shut on my fingers, and getting hung by the legs. None of the heavy stuff they reserve for the fedayeen.

I asked Kamous *why* they did that. He said the Shin Bet accused him of contacting the movement while in Lebanon and Syria. I said the Shin Bet then would have to arrest and incarcerate every Palestinian, because the movement is every Palestinian. He assured me that that was the whole point.

It was good in jail though, Kamous tells me a few days

later. He rations his story to me over a period of months, as if the whole of it is too much all at once. It was good in jail. It was very good. I met all the brothers there and I learned something about our condition and something about politics. We laughed a lot, you know. Would you believe it? We laughed all the time.

I do not know whether it should seem strange or appropriate, as I reflect on Kamous's experiences, when I recollect that all the Palestinians I have spoken to who spent time in Israeli jails always narrate their stories as if they were a joke. My friend, Fawzi el Asmar, the Palestinian poet who was under preventive detention for seventeen months and was beaten senseless by the Shin Bet, also told me that his time in jail was very "good" for the same reason that Kamous had. More than that, Fawzi el Asmar, soon after his release —under pressure from Jean-Paul Sartre and others—wrote a tender poem titled *To a Jewish Friend* in which he said that he did not and will not hate, that our struggle will never be against the Jewish people or the Israeli people or any other people, but against a system that has dehumanized both us and them.

Every three months a prison official would come in, Kamous told me, to read a list of names of those to be released. Every three months life comes to a standstill in our section of the jail. The official reads the names of the prisoners aloud and follows that with a pause, then either the word "detained" or "released." By the ninth month I had given up on ever being released. The next time the fellow comes around, I am reading a book. I keep my eyes on it when I hear my name and I say: "Detained!" What the hell. The man shouts back: "Released!" I say: "Thank you." What else could I say, at a time like that?

Soon after Kamous told me all this, and much more, the Israeli government sent a team of assassins to Beirut to gun down Kamal Nasser and two other Palestinian leaders in their homes. A picture of the poet lying in a pool of blood in his apartment was on the front page of the *Herald-Tribune,*

Figaro, and *France Soir.* A few days later, I remember the
intensity with which Kamous had loved the man and his
poetry and I tried to reach him in order to explain that I
too felt great anguish at Kamal Nasser's death, but I could
not find him. Kamous simply disappeared. I never saw him
again. But I knew where he went. Perhaps a man knows where
to go at a moment like this. Perhaps, if driven enough, as
Kamous was, he will find the way and get there. Perhaps there
are limits to the capacity of a man to endure rationality when
his soul has been trampled upon and his attempt to guard
what is left of his shattered identity is rejected by others
around him.

It becomes ever more difficult every day for a Third
World person to communicate the essence of his experience to
people in the West; not only because they remain so unyield-
ing in their attitudes, their myths, and their blatant racism.
Not only because he finds it increasingly urgent to return to
his roots and scour the culture of the West off his consciousness and off his back. Rather it is because a Third World
person's linear development, his idiom and his metaphor, will
forever remain alien to Western society. He is located in a
spatial and temporal reality where his sensibilities respond to
issues and feelings that to a Westerner are an abstraction.
An encounter with imperialism, for example, an experience
of it, is not the same as a politico-economic system theoretically articulated in an ideologue's book. Imperialism is a
concrete reality that he feels and senses and knows and is
affected by; and it touches on his life in the starkest and the
most real of ways. It is there for him to stare at and to bump
into as he walks down the street. It is reflected in the arrogant
faces of American "technicians" and "advisors" coming out of
their first-class hotels, with a look of contempt for his culture
and traditions. It is reflected there as they come out of the
air-conditioned offices of their corporations, oil companies,
and smart enterprises, with orders that must be carried out
so as to protect their economic and political interests, so as to
insure that twenty families, in a place like Saudi Arabia, will

continue to own 90 percent of the wealth and 100 percent of the power. And no doubt, for other Third World peoples, such as those in Southeast Asia, imperialism can be more stark, more devastating and more real.

So it is with the idea of the class struggle (or whatever other name some may wish to use for it) that rages around the life of a Third World person as if it were part of the elements. When I grew up on the streets of Beirut hustling my way through a few liras a day selling chewing gum, I was not oblivious to the sight of sheiks from the Arabian Peninsula driving their Cadillacs around town, staying at the Hotel St. George and squandering the people's money on their coveted Western gadgets and trips abroad while the people starved. The Arab factory worker, the Arab peasant, the Arab street peddler, who is not stupid, works in the manner of a traditional slave to avert starvation. And when he says "class struggle," using whatever term in his idiom to identify it, he is talking about a bitter fact of life, his own life; he is saying he knows that the resources of the Arab world, and the political power in it, belong to him and not to those obese sheiks from Arabia, to the moneyed families from Jordan and Morocco, to the well-fed bourgeois tourists sunning themselves on the beaches of Beirut. He is saying that when he rises up and does away with all this, as he did away with the tyrant Nuri el Said and the Iraqi branch of the Hashemite family, he is doing it as an extension of his concrete reality, his anger, and his violence.

So it is with foreign occupation. With deprivation. With repression. So it is with conditions whose essence to a middle-class Westerner will forever remain abstract. So it is with all these, and so it is with violence.

After twenty-five years of living in the ghourba, of growing up perpetually reminded of my status as an exile, the diaspora for me, for a whole generation of Palestinians, becomes *the* homeland. Palestine is no longer a mere geographical entity but a state of mind. The reason however, that Palestinians are obsessed with the notion of Returning, though indeed there is no Palestine to return to as it was a quarter-century before, is because the Return means the reconstitution of a Palestinian's integrity and the regaining of his place in history. It is not merely for a physical return to Palestine that a lot of men and women have given or dedicated their lives, but for the *right* to return of which they have been robbed. As the struggle for this right evolves and changes, the liberation of Palestine, in a sense, becomes the liberation of men and women. Palestinians, Arabs, and Israelis. The dismantling of Zionism, that oppresses them all, is the rebirth of them all. As such, Palestine is not a struggle that involves only Palestinians. It is Everyman. And in a way Palestine has always been that to the world. Zionism, an alien and transient neo-colonial system that implanted itself in our world, outrageously dubbing itself a movement to liberate Jews, but mutilating every liberal tenet in the Judaic tradition, cannot forever create conditions for Jews and Arabs to refuse to look into each other's eyes and see their own agony reflected there.

In the October War of 1973, the Arab peoples were not simply confronting an army of occupation in their territory; they were confronting the whole mosaic of racist mythology in the West and in Israel that essentially claimed that certain races are inherently cowardly, inferior, backward, and incapable of responding to the fierce exigencies that press on the human spirit. Not only was this racism shown in the despicable pronouncements of people like Moshe Dayan. Less than a year before the October War, *The Los Angeles Times* printed a political cartoon showing Egyptian pilots flying two jet planes upside down. The caption said: "We Arabs, we know how to fly sophisticated planes."

The Arabs, though not truly fighting a people's war, though not truly regaining their territory and though not truly winning the war, won more than any of these. They regained their sense of Self in the counter-violence they used to stand up to their oppressor. There is no doubt about how the Arab people felt after the October War. There is no doubt about how, microcosmically, an individual will feel in an analogous situation.

I do not know where Kamous is now, nor do I know what he has done or what he will do. I do not know how the Resistance can restrain crushed individuals like Kamous from their adventurist violence which does not help the cause or derive its authority from the wishes of the masses.

From preventive detention directed at silencing our voices to preventive welfare directed at blocking our aspirations. This is what the idea of a separate state for the Palestinians is all about as envisaged by the American government, the Zionists, and Arab traitors and puppets like Hussein and bourgeois nationalists like Anwar el Sadat. Not a democratic state that will be the first step toward the ultimate reunification of Palestine and of its two peoples in a secular, socialistically structured society; not a revolutionary state that will act as a magnet for the progressive forces within Israel; but rather a subservient, demilitarized province with a police force, a flag, and white buses that will come in the morning from Israel, pick up the workers and drop them back in the evening. (And they will "give" us this, "let" us do that, and "grant" us the other. They will even try to find some quislings to accept the whole idea.)

But all this we have seen before. From the time Hussein's grandfather, King Abdulla (whose regime and Hashemite family were grafted onto the region from distant Hijaz by Churchill), called on the Palestinian people in the midst of their Revolt and General Strike, in the late thirties, "to lay down your arms and trust in our friends the British to right the wrong committed against you," to the shelling of refugee camps in Lebanon in 1973, and to the notion of an artificial, puppet state—all this has been taken as a challenge to the resourcefulness and resilience of the Palestinians which has long since been proved.

When Kamous disappeared, I could never get him off my mind. When he had been around I took him and his friendship for granted. He always called. He always visited. He was always with us, sitting with us, slapping his knees with laughter till the tears fell down his cheeks. I had three other friends in Paris and they also, in their own way, disappeared. To me the nature of their disappearance becomes after a time no longer a problem of a personal dimension. When it crystallizes in my head, it becomes an existential statement about the Palestinian condition. It perhaps also makes a statement about the human condition.

One of these (for whom as for the others I choose a fictitious name) was Omar Karaman who like me was born in Haifa, the same year and almost the same day. We sit together to discuss a report "from the countries" about a clash between the Lebanese army and the Palestinian guerrillas. I am particularly disturbed, I tell him with emotion, about the news that the Lebanese gendarmes were standing at the entrances to the refugee camps in Beirut, including the Bour el Barajni camp where I had grown up, checking identity cards. I read another section of the report to him where it says that when the shelling started "women took to the hills with children tugging at their mothers' skirts." Isn't it ever going to end, I shout, aren't they ever going to leave us alone?

He says nothing. We are sitting in the Café Odeon in the Latin Quarter drinking tea. We have been sitting across from each other for the last three hours oblivious to the noise around us, to the traffic, to the babble of French students and the antics of street entertainers. One of these makes his living charming the patrons by scaring passers-by with a toy mouse that he takes out from under his coat at appropriate moments. Other entertainers come over to the Café terrace from busking the cinema queues to play their musical instruments or read verse of their own composition. I had a great empathy for one such street poet who may have been suffering, like some writers, from a permanent block—because he would come back day after day to read the same poem, a plaintive ode to the streets of Paris where, according to him, men and women walked around with masks on their faces not knowing each other, and how only he, and the streets, understood their true feelings, because he lived in the streets and would die, like the *clochard* he was, in the streets.

But damn it all, man, damn it, I say to Omar. Does not the suffering of our people ever touch you? You are so indifferent. So aloof. I have never known you or heard you to say anything, even against Hussein. He just stares at me with no emotion. He stares at me and says nothing. Then he replies: "It's awful. Yes it's awful." It is as if there is something in him that prevents him from summoning up any sense of passion.

Omar is always so neatly dressed. With short hair. Even a tie. And he is a veteran of the battle of Karameh and, for all he would tell me, other battles as well, including those before the movement came above ground in the vacuum that occurred after the June War.

That evening at the Café Odeon Omar interrupts me in mid-sentence to ask a question. He jolts me by saying: "I want to tell you about napalm. Do you want to listen?" I say I do. When a fragment of napalm hits your body, he tells me, it burns. And burns. And keeps on burning. You roll in the sand. You immerse your body in water. You cover the burn with your clothes. And it keeps on burning. The victim screams all the time and begs for mercy, for help. When you see a child hit by napalm, and you watch it die in front of you, or you watch it die as you take it to the nearest aid center, you are never the same again. Whatever dies in you as a consequence of this experience is never reborn. You are transformed as a human being, as a man, as an Arab, into something else.

Omar, at the time I know him, has visa problems. The Prefecture de Police refuses to renew his *carte de séjour* until he renews his Jordanian passport which had expired. The Jordanian consulate had taken his passport and "sent it to the Amman for renewal/approval." He never saw it again. But he continues to live in Paris without either a visa or a passport till ultimately, predictably, he is arrested by the immigration authorities and deportation proceedings are initiated against him. While this goes on, he sits in jail. And there is no bail in France.

I ring up Jamil Kurdi who works as a translator at the Fonteney section of UNESCO. Maybe you can help, I say, maybe we can help get the man out of jail. He meets me at the Ile de la Cité and we sit at a café to plan our strategy. There is no strategy to plan. Omar is in clear violation of the law. We drink more coffee. Then we drink café calvados. We get drunk. What can we do, I say. We order more café calvados. He tells me he is no longer able to work at UNESCO. Because I am getting fired, he says. Jamil is a Palestinian poet whose reputation is already established not only in Palestine but in the rest of the Arab world. He is fluent in Hebrew because he is one of those whose family never left in the refugee exodus of 1948, but stayed behind. In his apartment he keeps poems in shoe boxes, on the mantlepiece, in drawers, and in the medicine cabinet. He is also a full-fledged alcoholic. He drinks in the morning, at noon, and in the evening.

UNESCO can't take me anymore, he says. I may go "back to the countries." We drink some more café calvados. He tells me about his experiences as a top announcer on the Hebrew broadcasts of the Voice of Palestine.

At two o'clock in the morning we each take a cab home. Before he says goodbye, he says hey, we haven't done anything to help Omar. We have to get together tomorrow to see what we can do. I say sure, and get into my cab.

Omar gets deported to Algeria, the only country that would accept him. I go with Jamil and George, a friend of ours from the East Bank who is a student at the Polytech in Paris, to see him off. We hug him and he tells us to write to him care of the P.L.O. office in Algiers. For three months after that we all write long letters to him there but we get no response. We try the Institute for Palestine Studies in Beirut. We try other addresses where he might be reached. We never hear from him. I never see him again.

Sometime later the three of us get together to talk about the incident. We get somehow drunk, only George gets drunker than either me or Jamil. We talk politics. We talk about Israel and the Israelis. Jamil says to hell with us and the idea of a secular state. Why the hell should we forgive them, he demands, why the hell should we forgive what they have done to us, I say let them go back to where they came from, I don't want to live with them or have anything to do with them, my solution is drive the bastards out.

Suddenly I feel sober. The whole thing leaves a taste of ash in my mouth. I leave the pub where we are drinking and so does Jamil. I decide the fellow was just drunk but I also decide not to see him again. I don't see anyone again. I leave Paris.

Maybe Jamil has died of alcohol poisoning or dropped dead in the street. Maybe Kamous has died igniting an explosive belt around his waist while on a mission. Maybe Omar has died in a catatonic attack as he sits somewhere in Algiers recalling scenes of napalmed children he could not save from burning to death. Maybe George, who is a fascist at heart, who is already dead there, will go back to join the Moslem Brothers or open a bank in Kuwait. And when I leave and come to live in the States, I feel that perhaps I am also dead, or just alive enough to tell people that what brutalized and killed and dehumanized my four friends in Paris, as well as a whole people whose identity and inner terrors no one seems to know about, was the repeated doses of violence that have been injected deep into their blood stream as a consequence of their experience.

In Washington I give a paper at the Arab-American University Graduates Association about the alienation of the Palestinian in the Arab world and two people walk out in disgust because they do not want to know what it is like. I give lectures to American audiences around the country and they ask me racist questions. I read the American press and there are voices raised in indignation and compassion for the plight of the sixty-three Israeli prisoners in Syria. I tell people there are 13,000 Palestinian prisoners who have been in Israeli jails for as long as six years. They say, really, no kidding? We didn't know. Maybe Arabs don't feel pain. Maybe they have no relatives or spouses, and no sons and daughters and friends who feel for them. Maybe they are not human. *The New York*

Times, among other newspapers, seems to think they are not. When I first arrive in this country I am a patient speaker who wants to disseminate information, debate, talk rationally. I keep my voice calm. I am so patient. I am so moderate. Three months later, I no longer want to expose myself to indignities or contain my anger.

I think of Kamous, of Omar, of Jamil, and of George. Because they are the product of my own experience, I also think of myself, and where we are going. And when I do, I wonder what it would be like not to be a Palestinian for just twenty-four hours and explore that alien sensation of having nothing on my mind other than the mundane concerns of everyday life.

The struggle for Palestine and the struggle of its people for survival has always been in a state of flux. In 1938 the Palestinans rose in revolt against the mandate authorities in Palestine, and faced an enormous number of British forces and the treacherous machinations of the Hashemite family. In 1948 the Palestinians were deprived en masse of their patrimony, and a new generation grew up in exile. In 1968 the Palestinians, having supped their fill, ended their state of quiescence in the battle Karameh. Each uprising resulted in the Zionists having their day and the Palestinians their eclipse. And each time the Palestinians refused to be subdued or cowed, and Zionism, along with its racist and settler-colonialist ideology, was rejected, reviled, and struggled against even more. In its sixty-year history in our part of the world, this movement has received no acceptance from any state, any group, any political party or any influential individual. No one has come forth to sign a treaty with it, or in any way validate its existence. If the black peoples of South Africa, Zimbabwe, Angola, and Mozambique would not accept apartheid, racism, and colonialism, why should the Arabs?

The Palestinian cause has been characterized by setbacks throughout its history, but it has survived and become more universal in its appeal and orientation. Those who lead it may be assassinated, may be silenced, may be no longer useful or may be overthrown, but the cause remains and survives as a human and political one that will culminate in being addressed. The Israeli government, by killing three top Palestinian leaders in Beirut in 1973 and by murdering Palestinian spokesmen in European capitals may have hoped to go beyond the assassination of individuals to assassinate the cause itself by silencing those who articulate it and keep it alive. But surely the grievance of the Palestinian people will remain a case study of the violation of the human rights of a whole people even without leaders and without a movement.

In 1954, John Foster Dulles, while on a state visit to Lebanon, gave a speech to the Alumni Club at the American University of Beirut. He talked, of course, about the "communist menace" and "the powers of darkness" that were threatening "the free world." He also talked about the Palestinian problem. This problem, he claimed, would be solved only in time, when a new generation of "Arab refugees"—as he called the Palestinians—grew up in their host countries and lost their attachment to the land. It could not have occurred to him that this generation he talked about would grow up with Palestine more graphic in its mind, with Palestinian images and Palestinian active mythology more meaningful to it than to the generation that came before. There was a lot of ignorance about Palestinians and their identity in those days. This ignorance has not in any way diminished now. It is still reflected, twenty years later, in 1974, in the pronouncements about a separate (by which is meant "puppet") state, as if it were probable that a people that had been struggling for self-determination for three-quarters of a century could be cowed into accepting a solution such as this.

I once belonged to that small group of Palestinian individuals who believed that their political situation is a Palestinian problem that could be solved in a pure and simple way by Palestinians, by individuals, groups, parties, or a movement. This naïve grasp of the politics of the Middle East was reflected in the pages of the manuscript for *The Disinherited* as I was writing it against the background of the massacres in

Jordan, the so-called Rogers Peace Plan, and the machinations of the American government in the affairs of the Arab world and the destiny of its people. And my ideas so appeared in print.

To the extent that I described the Palestinian experience as being unique and having shaped the psychological make-up of a whole generation, my argument was correct. I was wrong in not realizing that the conflict in the Middle East was in reality a struggle for Palestine that involved all the peoples of the Middle East; that the problems of the Arab world, being as they are the problems of an oppressed people struggling against imperialism, indigenous reactionary overlords and for justice and freedom, are every bit the concern of every Palestinian; that every progressive person in the Middle East who identifies with the revolutionary left is very much part of the Palestinian revolution, and so is every Palestinian a true Arab patriot whose goals have transcended the parochial nationalism of the early days of Fatah; and finally I was wrong in supposing it is possible for us to compromise with Zionism even if this compromise would—as I had erroneously imagined in the past —somehow diminish or bring to an end the gruesome suffering of our people.

As such, one might say I am a person who has been in perpetual disagreement with the political strategy of our movement. At the time, between Karameh and the massacres in Jordan, I was advocating interim goals, compromise, and a simplistic trust in those systems whose feedback is always derived from oppression and violence. Later, between the events of Ajlun in 1971 and the October War of 1973, Palestinian spokesmen began to reverse their position and to call for the idea of a separate state ("national authority over Palestinian territory" sounds innocuous enough), thereby, as I see it, cheating the masses from whom they had drawn optimal resources and heroic resistance.

In a sense it does not matter now. The direction of the struggle has gone, as it did in the later stages of the 1936–1939 Revolt in Palestine, into the hands of the masses, and not into the hands, in this case, of the Palestine Liberation Organization.

On the eve of the so-called Geneva Conference, arranged for by the Americans to create an ugly peace in the Middle East not unlike the one that prevailed for the Vietnamese after *their* Geneva Conference, Yasser Arafat, whose leadership had long since gone bad in the teeth, became a groupie of the Egyptian regime. George Habbash, from his sickbed, continued to issue his rigidly doctrinaire views, and Nayef Hawatmeh, whose humanism and the rigor of whose consistent ideology had been established, called for participation in negotiations alongside the Zionists, Arab reactionaries, and the Americans in Geneva. Perhaps others will emerge better fit to lead, to guide, and to motivate the masses whose tradition has already been confrontation rather than accommodation with conferences like the one in Geneva.

In the States, I come close to the most racist society that I had ever lived in, including the ones in Australia and France. People do not stand on ceremony here. So I draw away from it and I begin to make Palestinian and Arab friends, as if to begin another cycle of exploring the level of mutilation that our psyche has reached.

I go to Chicago to give a series of lectures and associates of mine take me to an Arab workingmans' club patronized predominantly by Palestinians. They are mostly factory workers. Mostly middle aged. Mostly still in their working clothes. It is soon after the October War. Some sit watching a television set, talking loudly, and commenting on the news to each other. Others walk around or sit in groups conducting animated conversations among themselves. I meet a middle-aged man from Haifa who invites me to have a game of backgammon with him. He talks while he rolls the dice, about when he left "the countries" and how long he has lived here. He talks about Palestine as if it had not changed a bit since he left it in 1948. He uses the present tense all the time because the only reality he will accept is the one that stretches backward from the 1948 refugee exodus. He waves to someone across the table from us. "He is from Jaffa, this fellow," he says to me, and adds conspiratorially, "I swear to you by the Holy Book that the people from Jaffa, when it comes to money, are the most tightfisted ever. You know what they say about them? You go out with someone from Jaffa and when it is time to pay they put their hand in their pocket and come out with their money-handkerchief tied in half a dozen knots. Of course by the time you untie the knots, the check has been paid. Crafty devils, hey?" He says that and roars with laughter.

Halfway through the game, we talk politics. He says to hell with the Israelis. Let them go back where they came from or drop an atomic bomb on them. There is no other way. I finish the game quickly and walk away. Going back home later that evening I ask my associates about the man. They tell me the man's father, during the General Strike of 1936, used to be the conductor of a bus which was once attacked by the Stern Gang. Armed members of the gang climbed onto the bus and his father, in his simple, peasant way, waved his ticket punch at them, ordering them to get off. Instead of doing as he commanded, they dragged him off the bus and pumped him so full of bullets that his head was severed from the rest of his body. I said, that's gruesome. They said that's the way it was. Violence is not a new phenomenon in our world; it has gone on uninterrupted for decades. I said I know.

That night, in my room, I sat up for a long time thinking about what the man at the club had said to me. And in a weird and paradoxical way, through him, and through what he said, I was beginning to understand what was behind those equally despicable pronouncements that his middle-aged, insecure Israeli counterparts, who had survived Nazi crimes, made about the Arabs. I did not understand fully—after all we were not Europeans and we did not commit any crimes against them—but I understood more.

The last lecture I give in Chicago is to a predominantly Jewish, predominantly middle-class audience of a hundred men and women. I talk blandly for just over half an hour about the myths and realities of the Palestinian problem and I say nothing provocative. When I finish there is a lot of noise and

passion. People are shouting at me and at each other. A woman
wants to know if I would not concede that "all Arab babies"
would die of malnutrition and disease if it were not for all
the care that Israeli hospitals gave them on the West Bank.
Others have similar questions. What about "Israeli Arabs?"
Don't they have the highest standard of living of "all the Arabs
anywhere?" Isn't it true? Isn't it? Isn't it true that "the Arabs"
on the West Bank and in Gaza have never had it so good since
the occupation started in 1967?

At the end of the meeting some people shake hands with
me. Some people are so warm. A middle-aged woman hands
me ten dollars and asks me to "give it to the refugees." We are
both refugees perhaps, and maybe for just one moment, we
can transcend nationality and religion and culture and reach
out to each other. A girl with long dark hair wants to know
about Palestinian violence. She is earnest and touches my arm
as we talk. She cannot understand all this violence, she says.
She understands me, she says. I understand her too.

That evening I am offered the hospitality of an American
couple who had spent eight years in Saudi Arabia working for
Aramco and "who love the Arabs." Their house is a labyrinth
of rooms, corridors, and carpeting. I don't know what half the
gadgets in the kitchen are all about. Then it disturbs me
enormously to see a huge picture of a refugee camp in their
kitchen as well as presumably arty posters about our struggle
for liberation issued by various P.L.O. revolutionary groups. In
front of me on the table there is a cup of coffee and a paper
napkin. After a while I wipe my mouth on the napkin and
say goodnight. My host says he is sorry I cannot stay any
longer. I am sorry too that they should portray the suffering
of our people in glossy posters, hanging us up, as it were, over
their refrigerators in their ten-room homes in suburban
Chicago. But I do not say that. I just say goodnight.

When I fly back home, I find that my friend Kamal Bullatta,
the Palestinian artist, has sent me a painting of his—Jonah
inside the belly of the whale, holding his head in both hands,
waiting for the whale to spit him out. Maybe that is what we

are all about. We just have to keep on going, talking as if in a useless, impassioned soliloquy, with no one hearing, no one understanding, till we emerge from the inky, black world of the belly of the whale. And as we slowly work our way out, year after year, generation after generation, there is no other place for us to go but Palestine.

Cambridge, Mass.

Modern Reader Paperbacks

An Essay on Economic Growth and Planning by Maurice Dobb 1.95
The Explosion by Henri Lefebvre 2.25
The Formation of the Economic Thought of Karl Marx
by Ernest Mandel 3.25
Ghana: End of an Illusion by Bob Fitch & Mary Oppenheimer 1.75
The Great Tradition in English Literature
by Annette Rubinstein (2 vols.) 7.95
The Growth of the Modern West Indies by Gordon K. Lewis 4.50
Guatemala: Occupied Country by Eduardo Galeano 2.25
The Hidden History of the Korean War by I. F. Stone 3.95
Imperialism and Underdevelopment: A reader,
edited by Robert I. Rhodes 3.95
India Independent by Charles Bettelheim 3.95
Introduction to Socialism by Leo Huberman & Paul M. Sweezy 1.95
Latin America: Underdevelopment or Revolution
by Andre Gunder Frank 3.95
Long March, Short Spring by Barbara & John Ehrenreich 1.95
Man's Worldly Goods by Leo Huberman 3.45
Marx and Modern Economics, edited by David Horowitz 3.45
Marxism and Philosophy by Karl Korsch 2.95
Marxist Economic Theory by Ernest Mandel (2 vols.) 7.90
Mau Mau from Within by Donald L. Barnett & Karari Njama 4.50
The Military Art of People's War: Selected Political Writings of
General Vo Nguyen Giap, edited by Russell Stetler 3.95
Monopoly Capital by Paul A. Baran & Paul M. Sweezy 3.95
The Myth of Black Capitalism by Earl Ofari 1.95
On the Transition to Socialism
by Paul M. Sweezy & Charles Bettelheim 1.95
Pan-Americanism from Monroe to the Present by Alonso Aguilar 2.95
Peru 1965: Notes on a Guerrilla Experience by Héctor Béjar 1.95
The Pillage of the Third World by Pierre Jalée 1.75
The Political Economy of Growth by Paul A. Baran 3.45
Politics and Social Structure in Latin America by James Petras 3.95
The Present as History by Paul M. Sweezy 3.95
Racism and the Class Struggle: Further Pages from a
Black Worker's Notebook by James Boggs 2.45
Régis Debray and the Latin American Revolution,
edited by Leo Huberman & Paul M. Sweezy 1.95
Review I, edited by Frances Kelly 1.00
Schools Against Children: The Case for Community Control,
edited by Annette T. Rubinstein 3.45